SEX
and
RACISM
in
AMERICA

SEX
and
RACISM
in
AMERICA

Calvin C. Hernton

ANCHOR BOOKS
DOUBLEDAY
New York   London   Toronto   Sydney   Auckland

An Anchor Book
PUBLISHED BY DOUBLEDAY
a division of Bantam Doubleday Dell Publishing Group, Inc.
1540 Broadway, New York, New York 10036

Anchor Books, Doubleday, and the portrayal of an anchor
are trademarks of Doubleday, a division
of Bantam Doubleday Dell Publishing Group, Inc.

Sex and Racism in America was originally published in hardcover by
Doubleday in 1965. The Anchor Books edition is
published by arrangement with Doubleday.

Library of Congress Cataloging-in-Publication Data

Hernton, Calvin C.
Sex and racism in America / Calvin C. Hernton.—1st Anchor Books ed.
   p.   cm.
Originally published: Garden City, N.Y.: Doubleday, 1965.
1. United States—Race relations.   2. Sex (Psychology)
3. Miscegenation—United States.   I. Title.
E185.62.H4   1992
305.8'00973—dc20   91-47010
CIP

ISBN 0-385-42433-7
PRINTED IN THE UNITED STATES OF AMERICA
FIRST ANCHOR BOOKS EDITION: JULY 1992

10   9   8   7   6   5   4   3   2

This book is dedicated to
ROBERT RHODES
to keep a promise

CONTENTS

Introduction   xi

ONE
The Sexualization of Racism   1

TWO
The White Woman   9

THREE
The Black Man   57

FOUR
The White Man   89

FIVE
The Black Woman   125

SIX
The Sociology of Sex and Racism in America:
    Implications for the Future   173

INTRODUCTION

The central idea of this book is asserted in the following statement:

> . . . there is a sexual involvement, at once real and vicarious, connecting white and black people in America that spans the history of this country from the era of slavery to the present, an involvement so immaculate and yet so perverse, so ethereal and yet so concrete, that all race relations tend to be, however subtle, *sex* relations. (p. 6)

I wrote this statement in 1964. Twenty-five years have passed, a quarter of a century! The written laws, particularly in the South, that used to make interracial marriage a crime have been wiped off the books. But the *unwritten taboo* ("You aren't supposed to do it!") against racial "intermingling" has not changed one iota.

If anything, the inflammable emotions surrounding race and sex have become even more manifest. In 1983 news headlines reported the shooting of Vernon Jordan, former director of the National Urban League, for (and while) associating with a white woman. But only a few such incidents are reported in the national news. In fact, the abusive insults and violent acts committed against interracial couples in our daily lives on a local level are seldom brought to public attention. One learns of such happenings by word of mouth, from friends and acquaintances, or by chance, from being on the scene when they are perpetrated. In Chattanooga, Tennessee, a white woman was horse-whipped by white men for "carrying on" with a black lover. In Providence, Rhode Island, in 1987, I happened to witness a black man and a white woman riding in the back seat of a car driven by a white woman. Another passenger, a white male, had been let out on the corner where he lived. Suddenly two white youths pulled up behind the car as it drove back into traffic. At a stoplight the youths began yelling obscenities. "You fucking slut bitch! Fucking nigger filth! Did you like it! Was it good to you!" Without warning, one of the youths hurled a full bottle of beer through the hatchback window and shattered the glass to pieces in heavy traffic at a crowded intersection.

Repulsive feelings and acts of violence against interracial couples in public are not "isolated incidents." Such feelings and acts of hatred stem from a larger cancer in our lives. The cancer of which I speak is racism. It is alive and thriving in contemporary America. Bad feelings and bad acts against interracial associations are part and parcel of the sundry acts of terror and violence that are presently perpetrated against black people in our cities and suburbs and on our college campuses. This violence is but a blatant manifestation of the more "hidden" racism that seethes just beneath the surface of contemporary American society and pervades every institution and every facet of our world.

I want to emphasize that racism is an uncanny hatred.

It infects not merely the economic, political, and social spheres but the most intimate sexual feelings and behaviors of our lives. While racial hatred demands alienation, it equally demands emotional involvement with the biology of black people. The first focus of racism is the physical body—skin color, facial features, hair, physique, particularly the ass, and most of all the sexual genitalia of both males and females of the black race.

Racial hatred, then, is carnal hatred. It is sexualized hatred. To the extent that racism itself is alive in America, the sexualization of racism is a *fait accompli*. Whether directed against blacks or some other racial group, sexual racism, moreover, is the most degenerate and perverse form of sexual turn-on. White people like those in the above-mentioned examples who cannot stand the thought, let alone the sight, of racially "mixed company" are bearers of this perversion, sexualized racism, which seems to be inherent in racism itself.

In addition to the concrete discriminations and injustices heaped upon black people by both individually and institutionally expressed racism, white people are socialized—the culture teaches and they learn—to believe in a battery of superstitions and stereotypes about the *flesh* of black people. Racism teaches whites to feel that black people are sexually dirty, vulgar, beastly, unnaturally endowed, and promiscuous. In a word, blacks are felt to be biosexually preternatural. These superstitions and stereotypes translate into fears that become dynamic in the emotional makeup of white people, so that black people are experienced and perceived as threats to white racial purity, as well as to the white power structure itself, the government, the home, the family, and even the future of white people not yet born. Accordingly, white people develop an allergic reaction in the mere company of blacks. Sexual "intermingling" between the races exacerbates this reaction to an unbearable degree, resulting in violent feelings and acts against trespassers across the invisible and not so invisible "do not cross" barriers between race and sex.

Of course, all of the above is paranoia gone wild. But to the extent that people believe and feel these superstitions and fears, they experience a frightening vulnerability within themselves; "frightening," because the vulnerability is forbidden. They are therefore threatened by what at once excites them and yet assaults them with painful emotions. When all is said and done about the reasons for opposing racial integration, the bottom line is invariably a superstitious imagining of the pornographic nature of interracial sex. Very few white people can imagine themselves sexually involved with a black person without experiencing feelings of perverse titillation or revulsion. Anyone who does not feel the same is viewed with suspicion and considered abnormal, i.e., "sick," "filthy," "pathological." This is essentially the race and sex content that is socialized and ingrained in every white person in the country. Negative, pornographic, inflammable emotions toward sexual relations across the color line are as American as God.

The same holds true for American blacks. Whether in reaction to white racism or as a response generated from within the black population itself, interracial sex is frowned on by black society, particularly by the black middle class, although revealingly a noticeable number of them marry across the color line. A black politician of high standing in his own right, with a family name of even higher status, married a white model and was unable to get reelected to a judgeship because, it was said, he could not be trusted by blacks anymore. The same happened to a black woman office seeker who had been married twice to white men. When she married a third time, to a black man, the blacks still did not trust her. I was told that they wanted to wait and see if her color had really changed. By and large blacks believe that it creates a negative image when any of their leaders and outstanding persons marry "out of the race." "Talking black and sleeping white" is a familiar phrase employed to ostracize blacks who cross the sex and color line, and they are invariably branded as "traitors" to the race. When Vernon Jordan was shot, the reaction from many blacks was that he had "asked for it" by being with "that white woman" in the first place. Black and white people disagree on most things concerning race in America, but when it comes to sex and race they stand shoulder to shoulder.

The black people who oppose interracial sex relations most adamantly are the various groups of the Black Nationalist persuasion. The cultural, political, and religious Black Nationalists, as well as some fringe "separatists," recite the same "reasons" against "race mixing" as do its white opponents. Particularly—like white conservatives, religious fundamentalists, the KKK, and other freelance hate groups—these black groups espouse the philosophy of racial purity, social cohesion, and political correctness in their rationale for rejecting racial integration; both the whites and the blacks claim and fear that integration will lead to the destruction of their respective family traditions; both groups agree that interracial marriage is "bad" for the children.

Again, for these segments of the black population, when the above rationale is stripped away, the bottom line is an intimate feeling of vulnerability and revulsion. Like the whites, these blacks feel that sex across the color line is "dirty" and "perverse." When they imagine or actually see an interracial couple, they experience themselves as being with the white person, and they experience contradictory feelings of pain. They implode with a cataclysm of volatile sexual rage consisting of embarrassment, anger, and hatred. A young black woman stopped me and said that the cover on *Sex and Racism in America* had offended her, that she had refused to buy the book once she saw the picture on the cover. I ran to the bookstore and saw a new reprint of the book with a picture of a white boy and a black girl facing each other, nude from the waist up. The young woman was not angry at the models who posed for the picture but at me who knew nothing of the new cover. Her complexion was solid black, similar to that of the model on the cover, but a redness had begun to show through from her anger and embarrassment, which seemed to be masking an impulse to blush lewdly.

Many blacks cannot bear the presence of whites. They do not like the way whites smell, talk, stand around, or emote with their white airs; they feel uncomfortable, as if naked in a roomful of people different from themselves. (All the while the whites are feeling the same way.) The very idea of interracial sex irritates these blacks, and they cannot discuss it for long without "blowing up." The sight of interracial couples makes them nauseous, and they feel as though they will "go crazy." Consequently, they experience *hurt.*

Contemporary college campuses are excellent laboratories for studying the social distance that blacks and whites put between each other, in large part due to "hidden" anxieties of a carnal nature. On both predominantly black and predominantly white campuses, the avoidance of whites by blacks (and vice versa) is strong, often bitter, and always revealing. "I cannot understand how any black person can sleep with one of them," intoned a black woman student at one of our more liberal colleges in the Midwest. "I can't imagine myself in bed with one of them!" At colleges across the nation black boys and girls conduct "soul session" meetings whose main content consists of arguing the demerits of dating whites and the best means of deterring the few blacks who do date whites from their "treasonable" ways.

In general, black society and culture teach, and black people believe and feel, that interracial sex is just not right. Since sex is automatically imagined and projected onto any and all interracial associations, both whites and blacks, including many liberals, wish that integration was not necessary to foster racial equality and justice. Ultimately, like whites, the vast majority of blacks really feel deep down inside that sex across the color line is morally wrong and somehow sinful.

On the other hand, black and white people do marry, some just live together, and many date and have occasional sex. In one way or another this has always been so and will continue in the future. While the number of such couples is relatively small and their percentage in the population is negligible, both whites and blacks react with great alarm. This overblown response is due to the high visibility of and the intense allergy to interracial association in the racially sexualized mentality of the public. In a supermarket full of hundreds of people, a single interracial couple stands out like a pink elephant.

The fact of the matter is, people who trespass across race and sex barriers are *fugitives* in American society. "Fugitive" is a stigma that all racist societies stamp upon interracial lovers. Almost universally, they are seen as "fugitives" from both the white world and the black world. In public the eye contact they receive is more than liable to be the familiar "hate stare." Relations with their families are always tentative, if not nil, and friends and colleagues are noticeably cautious or over-compensate for their anxiety with patronizing congeniality. At the workplace white and black lovers do not often reveal that they are a couple for fear of innuendo, jokes, covert recriminations, and outright discrimination. North and South, working-class or middle-class, interracial sex partners must be forever cautious about where they go night and day. They are always fearful of the public and tend to engage in discreet avoidance tactics. They frequent only safe places of recreation, bars, and other haunts where interracial coupling is accepted and where people go to meet others of similar inclinations. They appear to be forever in flight—psychological flight and geographical flight. Collectively and individually they are haunted by the sense of guilt that society imposes upon them, and they are constantly irritated by their sure knowledge of being "oddities" in a sexist and racist culture. These stigmata—of being fugitives and outcasts from society—bring interracial people together as kindred souls who desire love and companionship far more than mere sex. Yet the supreme taboo of the world—that black and white women and men are not supposed to associate with, let alone love, one another—makes their love an unpardonable sin.

Because of sexism in black progressive circles, and because of racism in white progressive circles (including feminist circles), the sexualization of racism is made all the more impossible to avoid. It is also coming to light that sex across the color line is not, has never been, and never will be restricted to the so-called straight world. Many lesbians and homosexual men are relating across color barriers and finding that sexism and racism are formidable enemies of their relationships too.

Repeat: when all is said and done, the taboo against interracial sex of any kind is alive and thriving in America. I am now prepared to state—as I was not when I first wrote this book—that interracial sex will never be more than tolerated in America; it will never be desired and valued in and by this society and culture; it will only be exploited and employed for pornographic titillation. Only a preponderance of interracial sex relationships or large numbers of them throughout the population will humanize our behavior toward such relations. This, for the reasons I have asserted, will never happen.

Despite it all though, some black and white women and black and white men will always engage in companionships across the sex and race barriers. The ultimate reason for this is simply unknowable. Perhaps it lies somewhere in that wonderful mystery we refer to as the indomitable human spirit.

Oberlin, Ohio
Spring 1988

Through it all I discerned one clear and certain truth: in the core of the heart of the American race problem the sex factor is rooted, rooted so deeply that it is not always recognized when it shows at the surface. Other factors are obvious and are the ones we dare to deal with; but regardless of how we deal with these, the race situation will continue to be acute as long as the sex factor persists. . . . It may be innate; I do not know. But I do know it is strong and bitter. . . .

—JAMES WELDON JOHNSON
in *Along This Way*

SEX
and
RACISM
in
AMERICA

ONE

The Sexualization of Racism

More than two decades ago, a Swedish social scientist was invited to America for the purpose of conducting perhaps the most thorough study of the race problem ever undertaken. The social scientist was Gunnar Myrdal. As it turned out, he produced a monumental work entitled *An American Dilemma*.

One of the most interesting aspects of the race problem was formulated by Myrdal into a schema which he called "The Rank Order of Discrimination." When Myrdal asked white Southerners to list, in the order of importance, the things they thought Negroes wanted most, here is what he got:

1

1. Intermarriage and sex intercourse with whites
2. Social equality and etiquette
3. Desegration of public facilities, buses, churches, etc.
4. Political enfranchisement
5. Fair treatment in the law courts
6. Economic opportunities[1]

The curious thing about this "Rank Order" was that when Myrdal approached the Negroes, they put down the same items as did the whites, but with one major change—they listed them in the direct *reverse* order!

Today the same reverse positions are still maintained with equal vigor by both whites and blacks. While I am not going to charge either group with being totally dishonest, I am going to assert that neither whites nor blacks were or are being completely honest with themselves. For, of the various facets of the race problem in America, there is no doubt that the sexual aspect is as much a "thorn in the side" to blacks as it is to whites. Both groups, for their own special reasons, are hideously concerned about it.

The white man, especially the Southerner, is overtly obsessed by the idea of the Negro desiring sexual relations with whites. The black man is secretly tormented every second of his wakeful life by the presence of white women in his midst, whom he cannot or had better not touch. Despite the severe penalties for associating with white women—lynching, castration, electrocution—blacks risk their lives for white flesh, and an occasional

[1] Gunnar Myrdal, *An American Dilemma* (7th ed.; New York, London: Harper & Brothers, 1944), Vol. I, pp. 60–61.

2

few actually commit rape. On the other hand, the white man, especially in the South, cannot seem to adhere to his own laws and customs prohibiting interracial intercourse—he insults, seduces, and rapes black women as if this were what they exist for. A preponderance of racial violence takes the form of sexual atrocities against not only black women but black men as well.

In the North, Midwest, and West, where there are few legal barriers against race mixing, many blacks and whites suffer social ostracism and castigation for engaging in interracial relations.

What does all of this mean? It means that the race problem is inextricably connected with sex. More and more in America, everything we make, sell, handle, wear, and do takes on a sexual meaning. Matters dealing with race relations are no exception. The Madison Avenue "hidden persuaders" and the "organization men" of the commercial world are functioning now in such in all-pervasive way that virtually no area of social reality, no facet of our psyches, can escape the all but total sexualization of American life. In nearly every television commercial, in every fashion magazine, on the "center pages" of our newspapers, on billboard, bus, and subway ads, in the tabloids of scandal, on the covers and pages of every "cheap" magazine—there is but one incessant symbol: the naked or half-naked white woman. The scantily clad white woman is irresistibly enticing as the ubiquitous sex symbol of our times. Sex pervades everything.

The sexualization of the race problem is a reality, and we are going to have to deal with it even though most of us are, if not unwilling, definitely unprepared.

. . . .

A tall, dark black man boards the subway at 42nd Street in New York City. He takes a seat in the corner away from everybody. He pulls from his hip pocket a magazine; he looks around carefully, then opens the cover and instantly becomes engrossed. He turns the pages slowly, almost as if transfixed in and by some forbidden drug. There are naked women in various "naughty" poses on every page of the magazine. Their skin is white. A white man enters and stands beside the black man. Quickly the black man snaps the magazine shut, tucks it into his pocket, lays his head back and closes his eyes, probably to dream or to have a nightmare.

"I can't hardly sit by a Negro woman," said a white man who served as an informant for this book. "I can't be comfortable in their presence. I mean I get excited. They don't even have to be good-looking. I can't help but get erect no matter what kind of looking Negro she is."

I have before me the October (1963) issue of the *Science Digest*. There is a picture of a black man on the cover. The caption reads:

> The Negro
> HOW HE'S
> *DIFFERENT*
> WHY
> WHITES
> *FEAR* HIM[2]

---

[2] My italics.

4

Inside, on one of the pages, it says that the thing whites fear most about blacks is that blacks have an uncontrollable urge to mate with the sisters and daughters of white men. White men, especially Southerners, are afraid of the so-called superior, savage sexuality of the black male, and they are dead set against any measures that will lift the African-American's status, because they are certain that such measures will bring the black man one step nearer to the white woman's bedroom. Meanwhile it is a common saying in the South among white males that "a man is not a man until he has slept with a nigger."

Listen to the advice a black woman in Mississippi gave reporter John Griffin, who she thought was a stranger to the way of white folks in the South.

. . . well, you know you don't want to even look at a white woman. In fact, you look down at the ground or the other way . . . you may not know you're looking in a white woman's direction but they'll try to make something out of it. . . . If you pass by a picture show, and they've got women on the posters outside, don't look at them either. . . . Somebody's sure to say, "Hey, boy—what are you looking at that white gal like *that* for?"[3]

The white man's self-esteem is in a constant state of sexual anxiety in all matters dealing with race relations. So is the black man's, because his life, too, is enmeshed in the absurd system of racial hatred in America. Since racism is centered in and revolves around sex, the black man cannot help but see himself as at once sexually affirmed and negated. While the black man is portrayed as

[3] John Griffin, *Black Like Me* (New York: Signet Books, 1963), p. 60.

5

a great "walking phallus" with satyr-like potency, he is denied the execution of that potency, he is denied the most precious sexual image which surrounds him—the white woman. The myth of the sanctity of "white womanhood" is nothing more than a myth, but because this myth is acted upon *as if* it were real both by blacks and whites alike, then it *becomes* real as far as the behavior and sensitivities of those who must encounter it are concerned.

The sexualization of racism in the United States is a unique phenomenon in the history of mankind; it is an anomaly of the first order. In fact, there is a sexual involvement, at once real and vicarious, connecting white and black people in America that spans the history of this country from the era of slavery to the present, an involvement so immaculate and yet so perverse, so ethereal and yet so concrete, that all race relations tend to be, however subtle, *sex* relations.

It is important to see how the racism of sex in America has affected the sexual behavior of blacks and whites toward one another, and how black and white people perceive each other and themselves sexually as a result of living in a world of segregation and racial bigotry. As Negro and Caucasian, male and female, what do we mean to each other as sexual beings?

I am reminded of the way the policemen, during the historic march on Washington in 1963, constricted their eyes, tightened their faces, and fondled their sticks every time an interracial couple passed them in that mammoth parade. I am further reminded that when the marchers were yelling for F-R-E-E-E-E-DOM, for jobs, civil rights, equality of education, and the rest, a young black man leaped in the air and shouted out—"S-E-X!" Perhaps he was a "crackpot." Even so, can one be certain that he was not an omen for our times? I am not certain, for, I submit, that, secretly, for many blacks and whites, sexual liberty is as precious and sought-after as any other freedom. As the other barriers to freedom fall down, sexual liberty will become increasingly important in our society.

TWO

The White Woman

There was a woman, a southern white woman, who for years was plagued by a terrible dream, a recurring nightmare:

It happened at least three or four times a week. I was in a cave. I don't know where the cave was located, but it was dark, and I was always alone, and there was no way out. I never knew how I got there; the dream always started with me just *there*—in the dark cave—naked, and shivering from the cold. I would wander around bumping into the walls, trying to find a way out. Then I would feel myself falling and tumbling down what seemed like endless stairs, and I always landed in a pit. There was still no light, but I knew that there were people around me; I could feel their presence. When my eyes got used to the dark and I could see who the people were—they were Negroes, a whole lot of them, a hundred or more maybe; they were all around me, and they were naked.

At first, I always thought the naked Negroes wanted to rape me one by one. But then it would come to me that the black Negroes were laughing, were making fun of me, were dancing around, pointing at me, mocking me. And I would soon discover why: it seemed that my hands, both of them, were ingrown, were actually *webbed* to the flesh of my womb. And I had been born that way, and it was terrible, and I would start crying and trying to free my hands . . . and the wild laughter of the Negroes and their free, swinging sex would drive me almost crazy. And then it always happened—somehow, in pain and agony, I would tear my hands free from my womb, and I would be crying, and blood and bits of my flesh would be all over the dark cave. Right away, the dark cave would get bright with light, almost blinding with light. A strange thing would always happen then—I would look up and around, and all of those black Negroes—their faces and bodies, I mean—would be white as snow . . . and it would be myself who had turned black.

I would start running and falling and climbing back up the stairs . . . but there were no stairs, they disappeared or something, and right then I always woke up, hot and shaking, and I would have my fingers clinging tight between my legs.

A black man who is at least fifty years old, a black man now married to a white woman, told me of his first sexual experience with a white woman. He was eighteen at the time, the woman was fifty-three, and the relationship took place in Florida.

The man was hoboing his way from New York to Miami. It was during the Depression, and although he

10

had twenty-five dollars, he stopped off at various towns along the way to ask for work in exchange for food—he wanted to have the twenty-five dollars intact when he reached Miami. Just inside the state of Florida, he stopped at a motel and went around to the back door, as is customary in the South, to ask the lady in charge if she needed any work done in exchange for the price of a meal. She invited him in and fed him.

"I need somebody full time," she told him.

He explained that he was on his way to Miami, and all he wanted was work in exchange for a meal or the price of one. She insisted; she had so much work to be done, and besides, her husband was an invalid and she needed someone strong to help look after him. They reached a compromise—the man consented to stay a week. In addition to taking care of the invalid husband, he was to make repairs, fix certain plumbing defects, work in the greenhouse, and in general be an all-around handyman. He would live in a room that was above the garage and be paid a dollar a day.

Before three days had passed, you know what that woman did—one night she came up to my room above the garage and told me that she loved me, and wanted to know if I felt the same way about her. Man, I begin to shake my head and say, "Nom, No mam, I sho ain't feeling nothing like that." She didn't do anything else then, she just turn around and walked out. Right then I say to myself, "Man, when the week's up, you better get the hell out of here fast."

But I didn't get a chance. The very next day, while I was fiddling around with something in the yard, she called me from up in her room. She said: "Come up here this minute, I want you to do something rightaway." Well, I stopped whatever I was doing and went up there. When I got up the stairs that led right into her room—BAM!—my eyes liked to have popped out: there she was lying on the bed with not a rag on her white body. Well, man, you know what I did? I ran back down those stairs like a ball of fire out of hell. But by the time I got to the bottom, she was at the top, and she said: "If you run, I'll yell and scream and say you attacked me. So you best come back up."

I was trapped.

From then on she started coming out to my room over the garage almost every night. And you know what, I got carry away; I got to like it—I mean with her calling me "Daddy," and me only eighteen—I fell in love; I got proud as hell. A young black boy with a white woman carrying on over him like that. And she wasn't no white trash, either. I found out her family was connected with one of the largest manufacturing companies in the nation at that time.

Then one day some white guy, a traveling salesman from Chicago, stopped at the motel over night. The next morning while she was serving him breakfast—(she always served the guest meals, you know)—I brought down his bags like I was supposed to do. But the guy told me he was going to stay another night, and to take his bags back upstairs. The guy stayed a week, and after a week he was still hanging around. All the time she never came out to my room not once. I figured something must be going on. And you know what, I was such a damn fool, so young and stupid, I got jealous and confronted her one day about the guy. I told her to get rid of him, send him on his way; hell, I could put two and two together. She denied everything and sent me back to my room.

Then it hit me what I had done. And I got scared as all hell. Arguing with a white woman in Florida. Oh, my God, had I lost my mind! I made several attempts to leave, but she warned me over and over that if I did, she would tear her clothes and say I raped her and that was why I left.

Trapped again, man.

The only way I got out of that nightmare was to write my brother in Miami and ask him to send me a telegram saying my father had died and I must come home immediately. . . .

Two stories . . . one a dream . . . one reality . . . and like blurred profiles of Janus, both of them are interchangeable halves of the same nightmare—a nightmare that has neuroticized and split the sexual soul of the South and the nation for more than three hundred years. If—as I shall explain later—the system of racism and white supremacy in the South has twisted the white man's concept of both Negro sexuality and his own, God only knows what agonies and demons this same system has wrought in the sexuality of the white female, especially in the way that she conceives of herself as a woman and of the Negro as a man. The southern white woman, reared and nurtured in the tradition of "sacred white womanhood," has had to deny and purge herself of every honest and authentic female emotion that is vital to being a healthy woman.

From all indications, our sons and daughters, and their sons and daughters in turn, will be victimized by the American sexual nightmare. This nightmare began during the era of slavery, when the first light-skinned African-American infant was born from the loins of a black woman. When the first black man was hunted down by a mob of jealousy-ridden white men—and the black man's genitals were torn off for "raping" a

13

"chaste" white woman—the myth of sacred white womanhood became a reality.

One fact is certain, this myth was not created by the southern white woman, and it was not propounded by the black woman nor the black man. It was, as it could only have been, the southern white man, who invented it to salve his own guilt. In the days of slavery this guilt stemmed primarily from his persistent, clandestine activities with black women. Out of his guilt grew fear—if he found it difficult to stay away from the "animal" attraction of black women, was it not possible that his wife felt that same attraction to the black "bucks"? Something had to be done. Certainly, the white woman in the South had been desexed enough already under the fierce indoctrination of puritanical asceticism. The white man's fear and guilt grew, as time went on, to an intensity that made him look around for even more stringent devices to ensure the "chastity" of his woman and to absolve himself further from guilt feelings toward his wife. There were two psychological processes going on in the Southerner's mind: one was the deep sense of guilt arising from his cohabitation with black women; the second was his sense of immorality about a society founded and maintained on the principles of human slavery. Somehow the *entire* "southern way of life," sexual and otherwise, had to be justified. The Southerner had to find or create a symbol, an *idea* of grace and purity, that would loom large in a civilization shot through with shame, bigotry, and the inhuman treatment of (at that time) nearly six million black people. Sacred white womanhood emerged in the South as an immaculate mythology to glorify an otherwise indecent society. What ensued was nothing less than fantastic. In *The Mind of the South*, W. J. Cash writes:

The upshot . . . was downright gyneolatry. She [the southern woman] was the South's Palladium, the southern woman—shield-bearing Athena gleaming whitely in the clouds, the standard for its rallying, the mystic symbol of its nationality in face of the foe. She was the lily-pure maid of Astolat and the hunting goddess of the Boeotian hill. And—she was the pitiful Mother of God.

Merely to mention her was to send strong men into tears—or shouts. There was hardly a sermon that did not begin and end with tributes in her honor, hardly a brave speech that did not open and close with clashing of shields and flourishing of swords for her glory.[1]

Cash quotes a speech made at Georgia's first centennial, in the 1830s that brought roars from the crowd: "Woman!!! The center and circumference, diameter and periphery, sine, tangent and secant of all our affections."[2]

In his desperate attempt to whitewash the "southern way of life" from guilt and decadence, and yet to maintain and protect this very way of life with all its sin, the Southerner further developed what Cash refers to as the "rape complex." In the mind of the Southerner the word "rape" not only applied to sexual assaults on white women by black men, but to any attempt at changing what the Southerner called "our way of life." Cash, a Southerner himself, admits that ". . . the actual danger of the southern woman being violated by the Negro has

[1] W. J. Cash, *The Mind of the South* (New York: Vintage Books, 1960), p. 89.
[2] Ibid.

15

always been comparatively small . . . much less, for instance, than the chance that she would be struck by lightning."[3]

The hypocrisy and sexual immorality of the South seem totally to escape the discerning powers of the southern white woman. Or, perhaps, it is her very knowledge of these things that has driven her, out of a sense of guilt through complicity, to pretend that they do not exist, to shut her eyes and succumb to a mode of living and thinking that have all but dehumanized her.

As time went on, the southern white woman accepted the sterile role her husband insisted she play; she became a doll, an ornament, like a beautiful painting on a wall that is admired and given lip service by everyone but which is actually loved by no one. Lillian Smith writes:

> The more trails the white man made to backyard cabins, the higher he raised his white wife on her pedestal when he returned to the big house. The higher the pedestal, the less he enjoyed her whom he had put there, for statues after all are only nice things to look at.[4]

In the truest sense of the words, the white woman became *chaste*, and she was left cold and alone. Meanwhile, between white men and black women, "There were love affairs," writes Lillian Smith, "that made white women despair as competitors; delicate, sensitive, deep relationships . . ."[5] It is significant that even when

[3] Ibid., p. 117.

[4] Lillian Smith, *Killers of the Dream* (Garden City, New York: Doubleday Anchor Books, 1963), p. 103.

[5] Ibid., p. 103.

16

white women are married and become mothers, southern white men still refer to them as *chaste!*

Not only did the southern white woman push sex out of her life as a shameful thing never to be mentioned; not only did she silently give up her husband to illicit, backyard love affairs—she also gave her children to "black mammies" to suckle and nurture, because, according to the myth of sacred white womanhood, the white woman was above such "nasty" things as attending to the biological functions and needs of child-rearing. And in time these poor, abandoned white "ladies" lived to witness their sons and daughters turning away from them in times of stress and strain toward the black mammies for affection, solace, and human understanding. Lillian Smith says:

To these women their life was only a shameful sore that could not be acknowledged. . . . The majority of southern women convinced themselves that God had ordained that they be deprived of pleasure, and meekly stuffed their hollowness with piety, trying to believe the tightness they felt was hunger satisfied.[6]

It was in this way, out of the sheer necessity for sexual release and expression, that the southern white woman fixed her fantasies upon the most feared sexual symbol of her times—the black man. Her preoccupation with rape was (and is) not only a grotesque fantasy, but also an accurate index of her sexual deprivation. The black man became (and still is) the scapegoat of the ideology of sex and racism as it was (and is) accepted by the white woman in southern culture. While she did not actually

[6] Ibid., pp. 121–23.

lynch and castrate blacks herself, she permitted her men to do so in her name. And she enjoyed, as certainly as white men did, the perverse sexual ecstasy of hearing and knowing about lynching and castration. The black man became the object of mutilation in and through which white women as well as white men could drain themselves of guilt, fear, and inadequacy. The black man became the living embodiment of not only the white woman's unconscious sense of sexual poverty, but of everything that was wrong with her life and her society. Just as it became necessary for the white man to project the image of the Negro as a savage rapist to soothe his guilt, it was equally imperative that the white woman accept this image as a means of proving to herself that she was *sexually* attractive, if not to white men, at least to black "savages." Indeed, the southern white woman grew more "rape conscious" than a great many of the men. Her hatred for blacks became so intense that she taught it to her children, and they to their children, and so on. Today the hatred, stereotypes, and absurd sexual emotions toward blacks are just as firmly entrenched in southern culture as they were more than a century ago.

A few southern white women rose up during the early part of this century and spoke out against the atrocities that were being committed against blacks in their name. In the 1930s, for instance, Dorothy Tilly led the struggle against segregation and discrimination. The Association of Southern Women for the Prevention of Lynching was also very active. These women fought the Klan, arranged integrated meetings, and even sat down and ate with black women—one of the most sacred racial taboos

18

in the South.[7] There were also a few southern liberals—
white men—who spoke out, but they, for all of their
"liberalness," were afraid to cope with the terrible accu-
sation of "mongrelization" or that seemingly
anathematic question, "Would you want your sister to
marry one?"

So, for the most part, despite whatever progress has
been made, the southern white woman remains a victimized product of her culture, with nobody on whom to
avenge her sexual rage except the socially accepted
scapegoat, the black man. And because of this, when it
comes to the sex-race equation in America, the southern
white woman and the black man, contrary to what we
hear daily, are psychologically involved in one of the
most inextricable and exasperating exigencies that has
ever been concocted by history.

Few white women, and even fewer white men, will
admit that white women feel a sexual attraction for black
men. White people in general say that it is the black
male who is attracted to white women; the reverse is
flatly denied.[8] The white woman, they say, is in no way
sexually aroused by black men—and this in the face of
the stereotype of Negroes being endowed with certain
qualities of physical dexterity and bodily finesse which, it
seems to me, ought to make the black man downright
sexually irresistible. On the contrary—the whites say—
while these "primitive" qualities are the subject of much
condescending admiration and even envy, they arouse
only disgust and revulsion on the part of white women.

[7] Ibid., pp. 127–31.

[8] See John Dollard, *Caste and Class in a Southern Town* (Garden City, New
York: Doubleday Anchor Books, 1957), p. 166.

It is clear that somebody is lying; in fact, everybody, if not lying, is definitely hiding something. And what they are hiding is nothing less than the terrible truth: *Southern white women are not only sexually attracted by blacks, but it is they who are the aggressors.*

Because of the informal taboos and official sanctions against race mixing, the black man in the South cannot express his desire for a white woman in any way whatever. It would mean much more than—as in the case of white men and black women—mere ostracism and reprimand; nine chances out of ten it would mean the black man's death. This in turn means that in any situation involving attraction between white women and black men, it is the women who must make the advances. It is a standard example among black men, when they want to illustrate the absolute danger of any particular undertaking, to say, "Man, that would be like slapping a white woman on the buttocks in Mississippi!"

John Dollard has pointed out that if the white woman felt only revulsion and disgust toward the African-American, there would be no need for such strict social and legal barriers against interracial contacts as exist in the South today.[9] Explaining why white men (and women) categorically deny even the *possibility* of attraction between black men and white females in the South, Dollard states that "white men are unconsciously aware of the attraction but dare not call up the intolerable idea . . . consciously the whole matter is charged off to the sexual aggressiveness of Negro men, and in this way the complicity of the white woman is avoided."[10] Because of

[9] Ibid., pp. 166–67.
[10] Ibid., p. 170.

20

the harsh negative sanctions and the severity of the penalty, black men will not admit the existence of this attraction either.

It is a sort of unrecognized, not-talked-about conspiracy on the part of everyone. And this "conspiracy," this illicit, underground mode of contact between black men and white women in the South, serves to cheapen and render perverse any affair that takes place. There is an established pattern in the way a white woman lets it be known that she is interested in a black man. A Louisiana black man tells the following story:

I was a porter in the bank, and there was this teller who always spoke to me very nice; and when she talked to me she always stood up close. I knew something was going on in her mind and I tried to stay clear from her as much as I could. But she would find me and always want to talk, usually about nothing really. One day she came into the room where I kept my mops and supplies. I tried to get out of there right away but she blocked the door. She back me up in a corner and asked me did I like her. I said, "yes mam." She asked me then to kiss her and prove it. I said I liked her and thought she was a nice white lady, but I didn't mean nothing smart by it. She cursed and told me to drop that nice white lady line. "Kiss me," she demanded. Scared like hell, I gave her a kiss on her face. "Kiss me in my mouth." When I did that she backed away and began to laugh. I pleaded with her to let me go before somebody came in there. She said she would but that she wanted me to come out to her house on Saturday and fix her coal "bend." I didn't have no way out, so I agreed. She told me that if I failed to show I had better not report to work at the bank anymore. . . . Well, she's not a bad-looking woman, so I been fixing her coal "bend" and doing odd jobs for her ever since.

21

There are two interesting elements in this pattern: first, the white woman exploits the race situation in the South to "blackmail" the black man into becoming her lover; second, she reduces herself to a "slut" (whether she is or not) by having to use such methods. The particular "style" of approach may vary from woman to woman, situation to situation. Some women will be extra "nice" to a black man, will give him preferential treatment or make cryptic overtones in the way they speak to him; others may relate "off-color" jokes or ask him to relate such jokes to them; still others may "kid around" with him about his or their intimate contacts with the opposite sex, using just the right tone of voice to convey an invitation. If the black man "plays dumb" or simply refuses, then outright threat is resorted to. Another example will suffice to establish this pattern beyond a doubt.

. . . A Negro student who worked in a white home. Two of the white girls in the house made advances to him; he refused them. . . . One girl persisted and said that if he did not oblige her she would scream . . . and claim that he attacked her. He packed his clothes and left the house that night.[11]

The sad aspect about these situations in the South is that in every case the black man is "trapped." It is as hazardous to "go along" as it is to refuse, because throughout the duration of the affair there looms the possibility of being discovered or of the woman getting angry; in either case she can, to save face or to take vengeance, yell "rape." The best a black man can hope

[11] Ibid., p. 167.

for is that the woman loves him, or that she is strong enough to keep the relationship a secret (or to deny it) no matter what happens. Dollard cites a case in "Southern Town," where a mixed couple was discovered, and when the mob came the woman protected the Negro, insisting that she had invited the affair and it was not the Negro's fault.[12] Such cases are rare. Even in instances where the black man is "absolved" of the charge of rape, he must leave town for fear of murder. Neither the racist system in the South nor the white man's conscience can bear the open knowledge of a black man and a white woman being intimate. Not only would such an occasion represent a blatant challenge to the most neurotic facet of the white man's ego, it would symbolically, and in reality, constitute a direct attack upon the entire southern way of life, as that way of life has been conceived and maintained for nearly three hundred and fifty years.

When it comes to sexual contact between the races, the southern way of life has been, and *is*, one in which almost everything is permitted so long as such things remain undercover, both in the objective world and in the psychological world. Psychologically, hidden behind the conscious veil of segregation, almost everyone in the South is aware of the fact that white women are susceptible to the attraction of black men. Objectively, behind locked doors, in abandoned buildings, in parked automobiles under cover of night, and in numerous other situations suitable for clandestine behavior, black men

[12] "Southern Town" is the fictitious name Dollard gave to a well-known city in the South where he conducted his classic study, *Caste and Class in a Southern Town*, during the early thirties.

and white women act out their forbidden passions. Bell-boys, elevator operators, and other black employees in hotels throughout the South tell of white women who come and go whispering of Black Michelangelo.

I know personally that such activities went on in the two largest hotels in the Tennessee town where I grew up. Moreover, the women in these places are not all prostitutes or "Yankee sluts" who happen to seduce an employee during the course of his duties. Many of them are local women, wives of local citizens, who maintain suites in the hotels for this very reason.

Black women working in white homes are awed by the obsessive questioning by white women regarding the sexual behavior of African-Americans. These women ask their maids some of the most intimate questions, such as, "How often do you and your husband have intercourse?" or "Did you ever have a white man? Come on, you can tell me," etc. White women also demonstrate unusual interest in jokes and anecdotes about black sexual life. It stands to reason that these women are vicariously enjoying the imaginary sexual relations that go on between blacks; they may even envy them. "It is no accident," writes psychologist Gordon W. Allport, "that prejudiced people call tolerant people 'nigger-lovers.' The very choice of the word suggests that they are fighting the feeling of attraction themselves."[13]

For the white woman, "fighting the feeling of attraction" is predominantly an unconscious or a built-in process. Segregation, the myth of sacred white womanhood, plus all of the other ingredients that go to make up the

[13] Gordon W. Allport, *The Nature of Prejudice* (Garden City, New York: Doubleday Anchor Books, 1958), p. 350.

24

American brand of sex and racism, have distorted and vulgarized her perception of black men as sexual beings. The thought of having relations with a black man may be a revolting or an exciting thing. In either case, however, it is a vulgar thing, a perverse thing. Against the backdrop of taboo, of lies and stereotypes about the sexuality of blacks, theoretically the black man becomes the most powerful sex attraction in the life of the white woman. And this is largely due to the sexual myth that white men have made of the Negro.

In the mind of the white woman, the black man is a superior sexual animal. It matters little whether he actually is or not; she *believes* it because her culture has *taught* her to believe it. She also fears the Negro sexually because her culture has *instructed* her to fear him. Unable to experience the black man in fact, the Negro in fantasy becomes the center of the white woman's sexual life—she elevates him to the status of a god-phallus; she worships, fears, desires, and hates him. Oh, how she hates him! Everywhere he is in her midst, and she can neither embrace nor destroy him. Deep in her heart, she knows that she does not have to be protected from him. It is the society from which she needs protection, especially if she acknowledges her interest in a black man. Yet, since she cannot touch him, she *desires* to be "protected" from him, she *desires* that the black man touch her, indeed, "rape" her.

Suppose a white woman is fascinated by the taboo against the Negro male. She is unlikely to admit it, even to herself, that she finds his color attractive . . . she "projects" the feelings . . . and imagines that the Negro is the aggressor . . .

she develops an anxiety and hostility respecting the whole Negro race. . . .[14]

Or suppose a white woman's sexual life is frustrated. The black man is a ready-made target. Several years ago in Mississippi there occurred the infamous case of rape by "reckless eyeballing." The African-American was on one side of the street and the woman was on the other side. She screamed. What happened? "That 'nigger' tried to attack me." "But he's way over there across the street going in the opposite direction!" "Why he *looked* at me as if he were going to attack me." The black man was arrested, tried, and sentenced!

It is in this way that the Negro can, and often does, become the scapegoat for many anxieties that have little or nothing whatever to do with sex. Freud has established that many people who are frustrated or handicapped in their sexual lives tend to sublimate their sex difficulties by engaging in other activities such as sports, art, or writing. The reverse is equally true in the South —where white women are largely denied the means and opportunities of economic, political, and social advancement; where their lives are drugged with the boredom of false chivalry and uneventful days and nights. The most exciting thing that could happen to many of them would be to experience an "attack" by a black man. It is, I submit, a very "attractive" thing for the white woman in the South to have a man punished, to have him castrated or electrocuted not for trying to rob, murder, or injure her, but for trying to make *love* to her! I submit that almost every southern white woman has experienced, at

[14] Ibid., pp. 352–53.

26

one time or another, an intense desire to make love with a black man.

Of course, most of us never succumb to the urge to break the severe taboos of society; but just *because* of the sheer absoluteness or sacredness of a certain taboo, there arises in us a tension to break it.

Jean Paul Sartre has pointed out that the playwright Genet steals because he wants to get caught; but when the police come, Genet runs like hell. Similarly, the white woman is torn between attraction and repulsion, love and hate, sacredness and vulgarity, the beauty and the beast of black men. If she gives herself to a black man, part of the reason is that she yearns to be caught, perhaps less so in reality than in dreams. And it is this tension, this psychosexual tightrope, strung from psyche to psyche, connecting and separating black and white, that threatens with impromptu violence the lives of every man, woman, and child in this country.

In the summer of 1959 a lone, dejected white woman of twenty-nine boarded the Greyhound bus leaving a small town somewhere in the Deep South to go to New York. This woman—let us call her "Doris"—had never been outside of the Deep South before. She had been born and raised on a small farm owned by her parents. Her mother had died when she was fifteen. At eighteen she married a grocery store clerk. This marriage was without children and it ended in divorce. Later she "took up" with an accountant and they lived together until 1959—the accountant "vanished" about the same time a rather rich woman with whom the accountant was having an affair disappeared also. Doris had a tenth-grade education. She worked variously as a waitress, textile laborer, and short-order cook. She also "picked up" men for money from time to time when she was out of work. In every respect she was what is referred to as a "poor white," and she believed "all of the prejudice about Negroes that white people in the South believe." After one year in New York she married a black man.

I was introduced to Doris in 1963. My "contact"—a social worker who was assisting me in seeking out inter-racial couples (and who had handled Doris's case when she first arrived)—had arranged the interview, and had explained to Doris why I wanted to see her. The social worker brought her to the main reference room of the New York Public Library, which was rather deserted that afternoon. I shall never forget the shock I experienced when Doris and the social worker appeared. I do not know exactly what I had anticipated, but I know I had not expected Doris to be such a devastatingly beautiful woman. My friend, the social worker, had informed me that she was redheaded and "nice-looking," but that was the understatement of the year, and she was literally bursting with pregnancy. We were introduced; the social worker left.

Immediately I began explaining in detail why I wanted to see her, what kind of book I hoped to write, why I preferred to see her and her husband separately, and that I would have to ask some embarrassing, or at least very intimate, questions. I asked her if she wanted to continue. Doris turned out to be the most enthusiastic, the most cooperative, and the most honest person that I have ever interviewed. When it was over I escorted her to the subway, rushed back to the library, and, trying to retain the flavor of her speech, made the following notations.

On meeting her husband. He and all them other dock workers would pile in every day at mealtime at this cafe where Miss R [the social worker] had done got me a waiting job. Lord God, did they make a whole lot of fuss and racket. All 'em were big men, and Jimmy[15] was the biggest and the loudest of all. Well, rightaway they all starts in on me, kidding me 'bout how I talk and all. Well, Lord God, I knew they didn't mean nothing, 'cause they all like me and said if I keep my mouth closed I was pretty enough to be a motion-picture star. But not Jimmy, he made noise and all, but he never picked at me like the rest. He just walled his eyes at me. Why, I knew the man hated me cause I was white; and I sort of hated him too, he was so dark and big. Then one night 'bout closing time, he came in with this big bundle of pretty flowers, and was all dressed up like Santa Claus—he sat down real quiet like and begin to look straight at me with not a smile on his face. I came over to see what he wanted to order, and he order *me*. I said, "What you want?" and he said, "You." I got scared, Lord God. He said he was crazy 'bout me, and said how pretty I was and what a nice girl I was and he come, *came*, to take me out on a date, and the flowers were for me, and he would wait till I got off. Well, I became so scared I could have screamed, and my mind was saying no, but I guess my mouth said yes, because I heard him saying, "OK, you hurry along now and get through and I'll wait for you."

On dating and marriage proposal. The first time I made a stark fool out of myself. I couldn't stop from running my mouth. We went to a movie and I was so nervous I talked all through the motion picture. You know, I was trying to pretend I was calm, and all I talk about was how nonprejudiced I was.

---

[15] Fictitious name for her husband.

How I had had relations with a couple of Negroes in my hometown when I was a girl, and how I had nothing against black people. Jimmy got mad and told me to shut my mouth, I was embarrassing him because everybody in the movie was listening to me and was giggling. . . . We saw each other a lot as time went on, almost every night. We had lots of fun. People always stared at us, but nobody ever bothered us, because Jimmy was waiting to knock their faces in. Oh, yeah, we fought some. I was always saying things that hurt him—you know, 'bout race, they would just slip out. Once I called him a coon and he drew back to hit me, but instead he proposed to me. I fell into his arms and begin, *began*, to cry. . . .

On prejudice. Lord God, I was prejudiced as a jaybird . . . and I still got some of it in my blood . . . you can't just get rid of it just like that. He's prejudiced too, he says he ain't, *isn't*, but just last night he called me a southern cracker because I like to watch the Hootenanny Show on TV. We love each other, that's the important thing. . . . What? Yeah, I had lots of white men pursuing me. . . . Jimmy may be mean to me sometimes, but he worships me too. I've had a hard time most of my life. Never had anything good and solid that I could count on. But with Jimmy, we are getting ahead—we got a savings account, soon I'll complete my IBM training course. We going to buy a house in Long Island . . . we going to have a baby. . . .

On sex and race. I wouldn't say that . . . our color do, *does*, make a difference . . . we like it like this. I'm glad. . . . Well, yeah, a little, I might call him some names or him me, but it's love, not hatred . . . exciting . . . [blushing] I've always heard that. Seems prejudice to believe it, but I believe it . . . but Jimmy's a big man anyway, over two hundred pounds. I'll never stop loving him. He's got my goat. If he should die or we break up, I don't believe I could go with a white man again. . . .

30

The proposition that the *sexual meaning* of racial differences is perhaps one of the most powerful forces that attracts white women and black men is frequently denied by many people, noticeably Marxists, who prefer the "economic" argument. According to them, white women and black men are closer together in the socioeconomic structure of American society than any other two groups defined on the bases of race and sex. In the South and North, but especially in the North, white women and black men occupy more or less the same position in the class hierarchy—they are in the middle, the "squeeze position" of being pressured up from the bottom, while being barred from the top. A diagram will help to visualize the idea.

Highest Status Group	White Men	Ruling Class
Middle Status Group	White Women — — — — — — Black Men	Semioppressed Class
Lowest Status Group	Black Women	Oppressed Class

In terms of education, jobs, political power, money, property, and access to various other opportunities that make for higher status, white men have more advantages than any other group. While white women are in a more preferential position than black men, the dotted line indicates that the position of black men more or less approximates the status of white women. At the bottom are black women; they have less status than any other race-and-sex group in America. Now, according to the argument, the proximity or the overlapping of the status positions of black men and white women tends to draw these two groups together more than any other two groups in the status ladder. The economic and social pressures serve as "magnets" between white women and black men. Statuswise or classwise, black men and white women have more in common than anyone else. By consolidating their relative advantages, black men and white females can cancel out their disadvantages and, together, move upward more expeditiously than the other groups, which must struggle upward singlehanded. According to the theory, in this case the similarities and differences between Caucasian women and Negro males tend to attract rather than repel—the mode in and through which this "grand alliance" is achieved in lieu of status advancement takes the form of marriage between white women and black men.

While I recognize some validity in this theory, it does not appear to me to hold much water. It is too mechanical. There are economic and political factors operating in American society that might tend to pressure different sex-and-race groups together in a common class interest; but this seems more likely for black women and white men than it does for white women and black men. At present the available black men do not have enough power or status to attract white women for these reasons alone; white men do. Then, too, when a white woman marries a black man, the usual pattern is for her to take on his status rather than for him to assume hers. People seldom marry for such rational reasons as this theory would seem to imply; and even if rational forces are operant in the society, people, as far as intermarriage is concerned, have yet to act in accordance with them. For instance, the most *rational* move that black women could make in the South would be to agitate for the nullification of all legal barriers against intermarriage. This nullification would afford black women legal redress against white men who refuse to support their illegitimate children and to honor sex relations with black women by a marriage contract. This would constitute a real step toward revolutionizing the power structure in the South.

I submit that the attraction or motivation of white women, North and South, to associate intimately with blacks is predominantly sexual. It is a direct result of the kind of race-and-sex psychology that racism in America has wrought. Certainly the social and economic factors in Doris's background had something to do with her eventual marriage to an African-American. But it would be erroneous to generalize Doris's situation, for only a few white women who marry or become intimate with blacks have background histories similar to that of Doris. With Doris, there seem to have been racial, sexual, and personality factors which motivated her more than anything else. If, for instance, she was concerned purely with money, security, etc., she could have married any number of *white* men who were in a position to provide these things in more abundance than "Jimmy," the black dockworker. Doris herself related that Jimmy made her "feel like a woman" for the first time in her life! "He worships me," she declared.

33

The function of relations between black men and white women, as far as the society is concerned, may be political or economic (and I will come to this), but the *intent* of white women and the forces that impel them toward black men are largely not political, not ideological, and definitely not a result of the socioeconomic mechanics that are operating in the society. In fact, politically, and especially socially and economically, the white woman who steps across the color bar is severely penalized. She is ostracized, she loses friends, she may be fired from her job, she has difficulty in getting an apartment, and so forth. When we consider these things, it becomes difficult to understand why a "normal" white woman in her "right mind" would marry a black man. Against the backdrop of sex and racism in America, the white woman who becomes intimate with a black man desires that black man for *personal*, perhaps psychiatric (sexual), reasons of her own.

It is a well-known fact that when it comes to the "touchy" areas of our lives, the truth is hard to unearth. Even when people want to tell you the truth or think they are telling you the truth, such may not be the case, for the truth has ways of hiding and disguising its face. This is particularly true in the area of interracial relations. Not all, but almost every white woman whom I interviewed insisted on, among other things, the *altruistic* motive as the binding element in her involvement with a black man. Even "Doris," who was unbelievably candid and earthy, spoke repeatedly about love, the blinding love that took precedence over all other considerations.

This is not altogether unbelievable, or, at least, it is

34

not untenable. In most extreme situations altruism is often a potent element. When we consider the public laws and private sentiments against interracial relations in America, a white woman who becomes involved with a black man finds herself in a situation that is, indeed, *extreme*. There is little that is "acceptable" about it, statistically or qualitatively. In a white woman-black man relationship, the most genuine thread that can sustain such a relationship is, without a doubt, love. Altruism and love are not necessarily the same. But, from Romeo and Juliet down to the contemporary runaway boy and girl, one thing is incontestable: The quality that makes an authentic relationship between a man and a woman withstand the pressures of the world is *altruistic* love. Altruistic love is most frequently evident in a situation where there are powerful forces working *against* that situation (i.e., a white woman-black man relationship in the United States).

I have witnessed, not many, but a few couples that possessed the quality of altruistic love. One of these couples granted me an interview. They seemed so perfectly matched and genuinely in love that one runs the hazard of "romanticizing" them. They were in their fifties and had been married for over twenty-five years. They had three children, one light and two dark, all of whom were in college. The wife told me the following:

. . . only reason we consented to see you was because you sounded as if you were sincere in what you want to do. . . . We do not cater to reporters and other kinds of writers who want only to make a scandal or an "example" out of the fact that I'm white and my husband's Negro. We live a quiet and

3 5

productive life. . . . No, we do not hide from people or from society; on the other hand, we don't make an outside show to the world of our marriage . . . we're not proud, nor are we ashamed of our colors—we're thankful that we are happy and love one another. . . .

She later told me that she loved her husband not because he was a Negro, or in spite of it, but, "basically, because he is a wonderful man." I hesitated to do so, but I nevertheless asked her a rather intimate question. She cocked her eye and said: "Why, of course. I can't imagine two people being married as long as we have without sex being a part of the reason they love one another."

I have found that honest curiosity, or infatuation, may lead a white woman to fall in love with a black man. A white woman may simply become fascinated over the black man's color, over what has recently been labeled the "black mystique." The Negro is dark, he is kept out of the mainstream of the public eye—this makes him mysterious and lends a measure of intrigue to his person. After all, if she is not prejudiced, the white woman may find the Negro "exciting" simply because she has lived mostly in a white world away from black people. I believe that American women are prone to be curious about, or attracted by, foreign men (even Africans), because they find these men "exotic." To many white women the African-American is considered as a sort of "foreigner." Then, too, there is in us all, especially women, a *desire for new experience* that has the persistence of an inborn instinct. If a white woman is unmarried or unhappily married, she may yield, despite the social taboo against it, to her desire for new experience and embark upon a relationship with a black man. After all, in the North she cannot legally be prevented from or penalized for associating with a black man.

There are white women in the North who, because of their sincere identification with the African-American as an underdog, do not make a deliberate effort to exclude blacks from the possibility of sexual intimacy. Such women usually come from radical or liberal family backgrounds, and they themselves are often dedicated to "liberal causes": trade unionism, civil rights, religious tolerance, world peace, disarmament, female equality, and so forth. Many of them meet blacks in the course of their liberal or radical activities. Among the women who marry or who "go with" blacks, Jews and other "ethnic sympathizers" are markedly noticeable. Out of every three white women I interviewed in New York City who were married to blacks or who were intimate with blacks, at least one of them was a Jew.

In an informal discussion with a group of white women on the motivations for interracial marriages, one of the women ended with the following remarks:

I don't know about the rest . . . but I've been married once, and I've had several boy friends, both white and Negro. Frankly, the reason, or the motive, I married my present husband [a Negro] was because he loves me better or more than any other man that I've come across, black or white. . . .

If we adhere to the "love and cherish" creed of marriage, this would seem to be the best reason, or the "healthiest" motive, for marrying a black person—or, for that matter, marrying anybody. But, in a society which tacitly says that a white woman is not supposed to marry or associate intimately with a black man, no matter what the circumstances, can there be anything such as "healthy motives"? The important question is: Does the *woman* love the black man? And, even so: Are her *motives* for loving him "healthy"? It seems to me that the majority of Americans look upon any white woman who marries a black man as an "oddball"—the very fact that a white woman lets herself fall in love with a black man automatically means that the woman, if not a derelict, is some sort of "disturbed" person.

Of course, a so-called free and democratic society which views interracial love in this manner is itself an "unhealthy society." Racism penetrates every layer and fiber of American culture. No one is likely to argue that racism is a palatable ingredient in our lives, except the racist, who needs to be institutionalized. If there are "unhealthy motives" involved on the part of white women who become intimate with blacks, such symptoms of "unhealth" are largely the effects of an insane society. Thus, white women (too many of them, I am afraid) associate with black men out of a deranged, indeed, a depraved concept of themselves as women and of Negroes as men.

The apparent sexual effects of the black man upon white women in the North are in many ways similar to those in the South. It is in the North, however—primarily because of the absence of legal interracial barriers—that we see these effects work themselves out on a grand scale. I have stated that whites conceive of the black male predominantly in genital terms—that is, as a "bull" or as some kind of "walking phallus." To the pornographic mind this may be either disgusting or attractive, but it is always exciting! These two emotions—revulsion and desire—combine themselves in the psyche in such a way that the black man is perceived as sexually "abnormal." So that many white women who have intercourse with a black man feel as if they have been "raped." The man may be ever so gentle and kind; the woman nevertheless feels that he has "ravished" her. Indeed, such women *desire* to be "ravished," and many of them tell their black lovers that they can never "sleep with a white man again." The reader will recall Doris's appraisal of her situation.

The best example of the white woman's preoccupation with the black man's genitals as grotesque came to my attention when a white woman related how "surprised and disappointed" she was to discover that the penis of her black date was no different, except in color, than that of her white boy friend. The woman immediately stopped dating the black man; he was merely a normal man!

White America perceives—or conceives of—the American black man as a "clothed African savage." White people—men as well as women—want to see the black man's penis. They want to see this "clothed savage" naked. The taboo against the "savage" adds to the temptation, and the fact that sex with the black man is "forbidden" makes it all the more exciting, the more obscenely desirable. A young girl who temporarily broke off her engagement with her white fiancé because of a black man, told the black man her sole reason—he was a "good bedfellow." A black female informant who is married to a white man and who has several white women as friends, stated that one of these women explained to her why she continued to see a certain black man when she knew he did not really care for her—"I know he's using me . . . but he's good in bed, and it's worth it."

There are white women who constantly seek out black men to the exclusion of white ones because their psychosexual make-up, through repeated disappointing experiences with white men, has become so deranged that they can experience sexual satisfaction only with black men. Many of these women recognize their condition and sadly resign themselves to it. At an interracial party, one white woman remarked pitifully to another: "We both know why we are here."

Of course, being unaccustomed to white flesh, the black man may be extremely potent and very exciting on the love couch as opposed to a white man who is used to white women. No doubt this is the case in some situations. Be that as it may, I suspect that a great many white women bring to the love couch preconceived notions or expectations about the sexuality of the Negro; in America, everyone (especially the white woman) is socially conditioned to think of the African-American as "that" kind of animal. For this reason, some white women "play up" to black men in public or at parties as a kind of *threat* to extract favor or attention from, or to arouse jealousy in, their own men.

An African-American sociologist who studied for his doctorate at a white university in the state of Washington gives the following account:

Everytime I got together with them, his wife would oil all over me . . . right in front of her husband too. She always

40

wanted to dance with me very close up, and you know I never could dance, but she would insist on me standing up there with her anyway. One time the three of us went to Seattle and on the way back she insisted that I sit up front—she was in the middle. And she started bumping into me, rubbing her legs against mine, and bouncing her breasts around in my face. It seemed that her husband didn't mind, so . . . I lit into her— we had some drinks, you see, and I kissed and petted her and felt on her all the way back to the campus. . . . The next day she had a black eye. . . . She told me her husband had beat her and had made love to her like he never had before. . . . I stopped going anywhere with them. Shame too . . . because I liked the guy.

It is interesting to observe the behavior of white women in the presence of black men. (Just as interesting as watching black men in the presence of white women.) It is particularly interesting with women who have had little or no contact with black men. They either with-draw into a tight knot and look as if a bad odor had blown into their midst, or they overreact by making flamboyant body movements and patronizing facial ex-pressions as though the king of Arabia had descended among them. In either case they are disturbed, pleas-antly or unpleasantly, by the mere physical presence of the black man. Since the black man and his very black-ness itself seem vulgar to these dainty white women, the sheer presence of his person is sexually exciting.

Many white women *enjoy* "fearing" blacks because this adds to the "thrill" of being "overpowered" by them. They tell themselves that they do not really want to yield to the beast, but after all, the beast has such grotesque powers, how can the lily ladies resist. A thin, attractive

41

redheaded white woman finally consented to go on a date with a black man who worked in the same office that she did. The woman told the black man that the reason she had refused his invitations in the past was because she was "afraid" of him. When the black man took her home and bent to kiss her goodnight, he noticed that she closed her eyes and began trembling "like a leaf on a tree."

The fact that white people think of blacks mainly in sexual terms is brought out by the following account. A northern white woman was asked if she would have anything against blacks living in her building.

> I wouldn't want to live with Negroes. They smell too much. They're of a different race. That's what creates racial hatreds. When I can sleep with a Negro in the same bed, I'll live with them. But you know we can't.[16]

The woman was asked if she merely objected to blacks living in her *building*. Obviously, what was bothering her was that she could not bear to be in the same building with blacks when society frowned on her for wanting to go to *bed* with one! "But you know we can't do that."

I have found that latent or active homosexualism also plays a part in leading some white women to embark upon sexual relations with black men. Black lesbians are considered "men" by white women, whether they themselves are homosexuals or not. Moreno, the sociologist, has found that "homosexual crushes between white and Negro adolescent girls were common in a reformatory, for difference in skin color in many instances seemed to

[16] Allport, op. cit., p. 350.

serve as a functional substitute for difference in sex."[17] Indeed! A white woman who described her relationship with her black lover as "out of this world," stated that the difference in the color (black and white) enhanced the difference in sex. When I inquired as to whether she had ever had a homosexual relationship, she registered surprise and asked how I knew. She stated that a woman had taken her away from her husband (white), and added that such would never happen with her present lover (black). An active female homosexual from New Orleans came to New York, married a black man, and has been "going straight" ever since. Frequently when a white woman becomes friendly with a black woman or a black man, she may be either giving in to latent homosexual tendencies or fighting them. In either case, "black" seems to be the summit of masculinity—it takes blackness to bring out the "femininity" in otherwise frigid or near-frigid white women. Meanwhile, white men find it incomprehensible that some of the "whitest" Caucasian women choose the "blackest" Negroes in the spectrum!

Guilt, or a sense of self-loathing, is often among the ingredients that cause white women to seek refuge in the arms of black men. The source of guilt may come from any number of experiences in the woman's life, experiences which at the time may have had nothing whatever to do with race or sex. It may, for instance, stem from a sense of "failure" for not having lived up to the expectations of one's parents. Whatever the cause, this sense of personal failure eventually creates in the woman a desire for atonement, an unconscious yearning to be punished.

[17] Allport, op. cit., pp. 352–53.

The most "enjoyable" form of punishment, real or fantasized, may be found in a relationship with an African-American. Any white woman who associates with a black man knows in advance that many of her friends will desert her, white men will sneer at her, and society in general will look down on her. Perhaps this is exactly what she is seeking, what she *needs* to atone for the nameless guilt that eats at her self-esteem. She may also desire a more direct, carnal form of punishment from the very hands of her black lover. Not only may she want the black man to be brutal in the act of intercourse, she may deliberately or unconsciously cultivate sadistic tendencies in him. "My woman likes for me to beat her," lamented a baffled black man. "She cries and carries on, but never fails to provoke me until I have beaten her—then she's sweet as a lamb." Pining over a break-up with her black husband, an attractive white woman expressed her sorrow in these terms: "I miss my husband. These other men act like sissies; they're too meek and ingratiating." Such women as these often marry or become intimate with, if not the most uncouth, definitely the most bitter and racially paranoid blacks they can find. If it is true that some black men symbolically take out their pent-up hostility and aggression toward society in their relations with white women, the reverse is equally true. Some white women suffering from (among other things) racial guilt offer themselves to black men as a living symbol of atonement for the entire system of race prejudice in America. As white women, they "martyr" themselves to African-Americans. And—given the repressed anger and hatred that racism has created in the heart of the black man—a black man is more prone than anyone else to comply with the white woman's fantasies of rape and martyrdom!

In so-called "avant garde" circles, one becomes accustomed to hearing young white women who marry or "shack up" with blacks refer to themselves as "artists." They are painters, poets, writers, creative dancers, or they are "interested" in one or more of these activities. In reality, they are social outcasts. They have deserted their families, dropped out of college, run away from home, turned into beatniks, adopted the affectations of the "persecuted minority"—the next step is to go to bed with a black man. Not all of them, but most of them are phonies, psychological disorients, without true convictions or even the maturity to know what they really want. They do not understand that the energy driving them into the bizarre ranks of the misfits emanates not out of any personal commitment, or intellectual grasp of the "system," or unshakable dedication to art, and definitely not out of a felt capacity to love the black man, but out of a diseased concept of the Negro and, most of all, of themselves. In a very true sense, these young women (and some older ones) *discover* the Negro, but the Negro they discover is merely another stereotype, with his hair uncut and uncombed, usually "broke," talkative as hell but terribly illiterate, humming and shaking his head to the toot-toot of jazz music, mumbling ceaselessly about *his* "oppression," walking half-bent in an apelike gait or gyrating his hips to the "dog."

Deep in the psyche of the young, misfit white woman there is a need *not* for a Negro but for a nigger. For the nigger is a monster, a wish-fulfilling creation of the white woman's own deformities. By "deformities" I do

45

not necessarily mean that the woman may not be attractive; in fact, she may be very beautiful physically, which makes it all the more easy to hide inside of herself what it is she is feeling that necessitates intimate contact with a black man for its solace. Such women are known to pursue black men to the exclusion of white ones, not because they really think white men are sexually inferior, but because they, for whatever reasons, think of themselves as deformed. Therefore, in their minds, they are fit to relate only to men whom they also conceive of as deformed—black men.

It goes without saying that this also applies to white women who are visually unattractive—the ugly, the frustrated, the sick, the socially defunct, the perverts. I am not talking about whores and prostitutes, for most of them get paid for their services and render them to anyone who can pay, without respect to race, creed, or previous condition of servitude. I mean white women with jobs, even good family backgrounds, who, as far as white men are concerned, prove to be undesirable—a black man is the best they can do, and it is not the woman but the black man who frequently plays the role of the "prostitute." One woman, a schoolteacher, put it this way: "A white man can't do anything for me, or me for him. It takes a Negro to make me feel like a woman . . . as long as he does so I don't mind supporting him."

There are also white females who make themselves accessible to black men who are altogether different. These women are college students or young adults from good middle-class homes in the North and the Midwest. Frequently someone in their immediate family—usually the father—has made a name as a writer, a scholar, an editor of a respected newspaper or magazine, a government adviser, a social reformer, or even a big businessman.

These girls are sent to the "choice" schools. On weekends and holidays they journey to New York, young and innocent, inspired by their liberal education, to enhance their classroom experience by getting a taste of the real world. Most of them are naïve, especially when it comes to black people and the race problem. Their heads are full of theories and high-sounding principles. They recognize, however, that if there is one thing on which their liberal education and background has not really enlightened them, it is the African-American. These girls want firsthand experience. They engage themselves, while in college and after, in various types of social work among black people. They go to Harlem and live there, they volunteer to teach black children, they use the prestige of their father's name to acquire funds from foundations to set up various projects for the underprivileged, they go on freedom rides in the South during vacations, they march for peace, they donate their energies to organizations such as CORE and the NAACP. In trying desperately to *be* liberal and purge themselves of every ounce of prejudice, they do not draw the line anywhere.

I do not believe that these young women are insincere, or are merely out to "slum" among blacks. It seems to me that the majority of them are not satisfied just with liberal words or high-sounding principles; they are moved by a sincere desire to *live* these principles. They want to be free of all the subtle effects that racism and prejudice have instilled in them, both consciously and unconsciously. They want to do whatever they can to

47

make America a real democracy for all of its citizens. One young woman from an Eastern women's college expressed it this way:

I am not looking for a Negro to marry or to have sexual intercourse with. A girl cannot help being curious about Negroes, just as she would be curious about any man. But my main purpose is to get to *know* the Negro; we liberals and do-gooders are too often accustomed to helping the Negro with our noses turned up, as if we were doing charity work among derelicts. Integration is a two-way process. . . . Without giving up my own background I want to behave around Negroes in no way different from the way I would behave around whites. . . . And if I should happen to fall in love with a Negro or be sexually attracted to him, I do not see why I shouldn't marry or have sex with him like I would with any white boy. . . . I cannot be true to myself and draw the line at love because of skin color. . . .

On the other hand, it is not too rare to find young white women "using" their liberal ideas as an *excuse* to "slum" among blacks. Despite whatever efforts they exert to bring about justice and equality for black people, such women are deluding no one but themselves, for even they know that having sex with a black man is not going to solve the race problem—although it might "solve" the woman's problem. Many white women who have personal problems of a sexual nature become associated with liberal activities for but one purpose: to fraternize with black men. An African-American informant who has a long history of "leftist" activities, and who has had two white wives, stated that among such women having sex with a black man seemed to be viewed as the only way of "proving" oneself. The informant went on

48

to say that the older women (who had "proved" themselves incessantly) tended to exert pressure on the younger ones, especially the ones from reactionary backgrounds, so that he found it relatively easy with the help of the older women to be intimate with almost any woman he desired. Indeed, the older women seemed to enjoy pressuring the younger ones. The implications of this are obvious. In Ralph Ellison's novel *Invisible Man* there is a scene in which a white woman is procured for the black hero by the woman's husband. Indignantly the black man stalks out of the apartment, grumbling to himself, "You can't get to my intellect through my gonads."

With some white girls from wealthy liberal backgrounds, it is adolescent rebellion against that background rather than any real desire to obliterate prejudice and segregation that seems to account for their intimacy with blacks. Becoming intimate with a black man frequently represents defiance of parental control, usually of a domineering, successful father. Associating with blacks and supporting African-American causes is a form of escape from a background so far removed from that of most blacks that the liberal white girl is apt to feel guilty about it. The futility and immaturity of this kind of defiance is revealed by the fact that most of these girls eventually "wake up" to themselves, return to their families, and take up the kind of lives that are consistent with their backgrounds. Commenting on this, a young black man remarked, "These chicks are trying to escape from what they will inevitably return to."

A number of these girls first get the desire to have sexual intercourse with a black man through a kind of contagion. They know someone who is intimate with a black man, perhaps a close friend. Sometimes he is "passed around," like a stud, from friend to friend. Sometimes the girl waits until her friend is not around and then prevails upon the black man. The pattern is somehow reminiscent of the southern idea that a man is not a man until he has slept with a black woman.

Fabrications and stereotypes prevail and persist in our popular views of *all* blacks. The white woman, living in a segregated world, has little alternative but to accept some of these. She may be unprejudiced about all other aspects of the Negro, but when it comes to his sexuality, racial myths govern her perception of him. Indeed, the racial stereotypes of physical coordination, virility, dexterity, and crude emotionalism *constitute* her sexual perception of the black man. For this reason the white woman who becomes intimate with a black man cannot altogether escape the racial meaning of the relationship, no matter how unprejudiced she may be. In fact, it is the racial meaning of Negro sexuality, in all of its pornography, that the white woman *expects* and *demands* when she becomes intimate with a black man.

Repeatedly black informants have reported that during the act of intercourse their white mates frequently utter the most racially vulgar and offensive epithets conceivable, such as, "Rape me, nigger, rape me!" A highly imaginative white informant stated that during intercourse she often thought of her black lover as a "big black train" that roared down on her with piston ablaze as if she were a "long, descending mountain." White women who deny that racism in America influences the meaning of sexual intercourse with a black man are hid-

ing much more than their counterparts who say otherwise.

The myth of Negro sexuality, along with the other
stereotypes about the Negro's mode of existence, have
affected American white women to the extent that many
of them secretly envy or despise black females. The
black woman is denied virtually all of the "privileges and
graces" of American culture, but according to the myth
of Negro sexhood, it is the black woman who is endowed
with an irresistible sexual attraction and enjoys the sex
act more than any other creature on earth. To white
women, especially liberated ones in the North, it matters
little if such qualities are viewed as "savage and promiscuous," or that these notions about the black female are
largely false or, at best, culturally determined rather than
racially inherent. White women accept them as facts.
Some not only envy black females but actually want to *be*
black.

"Secretly I have caught myself wishing I were a Negro," said one of the most beautiful white women I have
seen. "Negro women dance so well, so sexy. And they
have so much soul, so much sex expression in their body
movements and facial expression." This is one of the
reasons that some white vocalists try to sing in a style
similar to that of blacks.

One finds in the North, scattered here and there, a
few white women—old and young—who have adopted
every characteristic, real as well as stereotyped, of the
African-American, from patterns of speech down to the
very style of walking. It is, to say the least, amazing to
see this phenomenon—the *white-Negro woman*. She has
that "gyrating gait," that bouncing of the shoulders as

she talks, that slur in the voice, that earthy twirl in her pelvis when she dances, that black-like contempt for whites. She is thoroughly aware of every injustice committed against the African-American, she can sing along with Lead Belly, Ray Charles, Billie Holiday, Muddy Waters and Mahalia Jackson as well as any black person. She knows who Nat Turner, Sojourner Truth, and Fred Douglass were. Her vocabulary is conspicuously incomprehensible to white people, for she can speak the "ethnic" language as well as any African-American, maybe better, and she has had the kind of organic intimacy with blacks—men and women—that has made her know them as well as, if not far better than, they know themselves. *Soul* is what she has. Unlike the liberal white woman, she does not watch her tongue among blacks. She will call a black person a "nigger" with the same intimacy and warmth or self-hostility that any African-American would. In every way possible—except skin color—she has *assimilated* into the black world both physically and psychologically. Sometimes she is a rejected white trying to find a place among other rejects. Other times she is *real*, perhaps more real than the African-American himself. Blacks who know her, talk and act around her as they do when she is not present. She knows all secrets, she shares all guilt, she enjoys and suffers whatever black people enjoy and suffer. In many ways she has out-Negroed the Negro. And if she is "sick and disturbed," the bulk of blame must be laid at the doors of a civilization that preaches brotherhood, humanity, and love, while it perpetuates in the field of race relations an intricate network of social, political, economic, and moral evils that make it impossible for any American—black or white—to grow up fully sane.

While the "white-Negro woman" is a rare and extreme type, it is not uncommon for a white woman who marries a black man to assume, on one level or another, some of the characteristics and preoccupations of the black world. After all, it is by and large the woman who marries into the black world, and not vice versa. More or less abandoned by white society in general, she moves within a close circle of friends consisting mostly of blacks and a few whites who do not disapprove of her marriage. The white woman, seeking to win approval from the race of her husband, automatically begins to adopt so-called black ways or African-American subcultural patterns of social etiquette. Except in rare instances, she becomes intensely race-conscious. If she does not actually become involved in the struggle for equality, she usually contributes money and sympathy to the cause. She tries to learn the subtleties of black communication, to appreciate the whole gamut of African-American culture, to adopt a "black outlook" toward the world. And she must forever keep her guard up lest she be insulted by jealous black women or by black men who look upon any white woman with a black as fair game for all blacks. This "slut concept," common to the men of both races, weighs heavily upon any white woman who marries a black man.

This makes it the more surprising that psychologists, sociologists, and psychiatrists have failed to unearth any evidence to suggest that white women who marry blacks are any more "disturbed" than any other women in our society. On the contrary, most of these women appear to lead healthy lives, politically and sexually; they become engaged in worthwhile activities—unless one believes that spending one's energies on the effort to remove racial inequalities is a sign of "sickness."

If one of the factors that attracts a man towards a woman is her sex appeal, then certainly, against the backdrop of our rapidly changing sex mores, one of the features that motivates a woman towards a man is the man's sex appeal.[18] The African-American has sex appeal, *plus*—even the white man agrees to this! It seems altogether "healthy," then, for a white woman to seek out a man who she thinks can satisfy, among other things, her sexual desires. If marrying a black man is "abnormal," it is so because the society makes it that way, and not necessarily the woman or the black man. Every black informant to whom I put the question, *On the basis of your experience do you consider your white wife (or lover) sexually restrained?* answered, "No." And when I inquired as to the difference in bizarre sexual practices between black women and white women, the replies were that there was no categorical difference. "It's personal from woman to woman and not racial," said one informant whom I considered more than competent to know. "Actually, white women and black women are becoming more and more the same," he went on. "White men think black women are more free in sex than white women. . . . Negro men think white women are more free in sex than black women. . . . I doubt it all. It's because of segregation. It's because of what we *think* and not what really *is.*"

[18] See "Sex in the U.S.: Mores & Morality," *Time*, January 24, 1964.

It is for this reason, I submit—because of what we *think*, because of an *abnormal* society—that the very hostilities of the outside world sometimes tend to weld together, in love and compatibility, a white woman and a black man more tenaciously than most of us are wont to surmise.

THREE

The Black Man

I am not absolutely certain at what age I became conscious of my color as a limitation on where I could go, sit, or with whom I could associate. I think it was during my seventh year, for that was when I received my first beating for associating with a white female.

I know I was quite young, because the incident occurred in connection with my long hikes from grammar school, which was about four miles from my house. After traveling half the distance the other black children would gradually break off and go their separate ways. I would walk the rest of the way to my house alone. One afternoon, I met another child who had books and was about my age, or at least my size. At first, we did not say anything. But as the days went on, we began to talk to each other, we became friends and made a habit of meeting at the intersection of our similar yet different routes home. Every afternoon we romped up and down the street. I think we argued once—about what I do not recall. I know I hit her because of the argument. She cried. I apologized. After that we became greater friends.

One day my grandmother appeared on the sidewalk before us. I did not know where she came from. She seemed just to *be* there, and, although I did not know what the trouble was, I sensed from the look on her face that something was terribly wrong. My grandmother, who was not yet fifty, caught me by the back of my collar, and literally dragged me all the way home. She did not speak a word. At home, she gave me the beating of my life. I yelled and kicked, and I did not know what I had done . . . yet, I think, on some level of consciousness, I knew that it had something to do with my friend. When Grandmother finished lashing my backside with her belt, bubbles of perspiration stood on her hot, black face. Then she began to lash me with her tongue.

"Boy, is you done gone clean out of your mind!" There was terror in her eyes, and I looked at her dumbly.

"Do you want to git yoself lynched! Messing round wit a *white* gurl! A little, trashy, white heifer. Do you want to git me kilt! Git all the colored folks slaughtered . . ."

On and on she went. Her words put a fear into me that I have never forgotten—the same fear that was instilled so deeply in her that, as she talked, her whole body trembled. I began to tremble also; for, I believe, at that moment I was awakened to a vital part of me that somehow I would have to kill. And it was then, only then, that I began to cry.

No white person knows, really knows, how it is to grow up as a black boy in the South. The taboo of the white woman eats into the psyche, erodes away significant portions of boyhood sexual development, alters the total concept of masculinity, and creates in the black male a hidden ambivalence towards all women, black as well as white.

I do not know if other black boys had the fear of the white woman instilled in their minds through as shocking an incident as I. I do know that they learned it. The particular incident may vary from black male to black male, but the lesson is the same: avoid the woman that is white, act as if she does not exist. I learned as a boy, and later as a man, to bow and avert my eyes whenever talking to a white woman. In the South a black man never looks a white woman straight in the face, never marvels at her figure no matter how attractive she is. On buses, in stores, on crowded streets, the African-American, at all costs, must avoid physical contact with white flesh. In Mississippi and other places in the Deep South, it is reported jokingly that a black person must step off the sidewalk when a white woman approaches. This is not far from the truth. I know for a fact that it is dangerous in the South for a black man to be caught (arrested, for instance) with a photograph of a white female in his possession. It would take a lot of nerve for a black man to express his admiration for a movie star (Marilyn

Monroe, Sophia Loren, etc.) in the company of a southern white man. John Dollard, in *Caste and Class in a Southern Town*, tells of an incident where a Negro was afraid to receive a simple letter from a white woman. Even in the North, as I shall show in more detail later, the black man's fear of the consequences of being familiar with a white woman is not unusual.

Because he must act like a eunuch when it comes to white women, there arises within the black man an undefined sense of dread and self-mutilation. Psychologically he experiences himself as castrated.

If a black man acts differently, he runs the risk of being jailed, beaten, or lynched. Nevertheless, many blacks run this risk. In secrecy, among themselves in pool rooms, on street corners, late at night when no white person is around, you can hear black men and teen-agers whispering and sometimes talking aloud about their adventures with white women. Each man who tells a story is laughed at, rebuffed, and "put down." The talk swirls as in a childhood fantasy. Yet every man knows that not all of the stories are lies or pure wishful thinking. Too often the news leaks out about a chauffeur caught redhanded, a handyman escaped North, a teen-ager lynched or electrocuted. Always the crime is "rape," but everybody, especially the white women, rich or "poor trash," knows better.

I do not propose to evaluate the singular, long-range effects of the beating my grandmother gave me as a result of associating with a white girl. How can I? So much has taken place since then, both *to* me and *in* me. I know this: had my grandmother not discovered my particular transgression against the ethics of segregation when she did, it would have been only a matter of time before someone else would have noticed, and the consequence might or might not have been as severe as a beating. What was important for me—as it is for every black boy in the South—was that I gradually learned to fear and hate white girls. My hatred was as immobile as my fear. I feared and hated without understanding. The thought as well as the sight of a white woman completely awed me, and since I knew the white woman was taboo, although not precisely why, an ominous gloom settled upon my mood and lingered throughout my early life.

I remember, during the Depression, standing with my grandmother in long, endless lines with other black folks, waiting for hours, day in and day out, and never reaching the doors of the building inside of which potatoes and fatback meat were being issued. All the while the white women and their children were moving up and onward. When at last, after our legs and faces were frozen from standing all day, and we were inside, the white women behind the counter (who were merely teen-age girls) would tell Grandmother that there was no food. They were arrogant, flippant, and would usher us back out in the cold, empty-handed. Tears would hang in Grandmother's eyes as she would begin to moan the old spiritual about being "A Stranger in Dis Land." And that would seem to comfort her. It did not comfort me.

I knew that my grandmother knew that those girls were lying. There was food, and it was being given to the white women who pushed and shoved us around. I knew Grandmother was a proud, self-willed woman, and I could not understand why she belittled herself before those nasty, lying white girls. I hated those girls. I hated all white women. More important, there arose in me an incipient resentment towards my grandmother, indeed, towards all black women—because I could not help but compare them with white women, and in all phases of public life it was the black female who bowed her head and tucked her tail between her legs like a little black puppy.

I think now—no, I *know* now—that this is one of the reasons black women encounter so much frustration with their men. Living in a society where the objective social position and the reputed virtues of white women smother whatever worth black women may have, the black man is put to judging his women by what he sees and imagines the white woman is. A common expression among black men when anything goes wrong between them and their women is to say that a white woman would act differently. Without ever having associated with, let alone having been married to, a white woman, the black man asserts, half-heartedly but significantly, that black women are hell to get along with! The fact that this may be said about all American women does little to alter the black man's depreciatory concept of black females. How can it? For the myth of white womanhood has soaked into the African-American's skin. In matters of beauty, manners, social graces, and womanly virtues, the white woman is elevated by American society to the status of a near goddess. Everywhere, the African-American hears about and sees these nymphlike creatures. The African-American's world is thoroughly invaded by the white woman—the mass media, newspapers, magazines, radio, and especially television, bring these lily sirens into the blackness of the African-American's home and mind. It becomes all but impossible for the black man to separate his view of the *ideal* woman from that of the *white* woman. He may do it intellectually, cognitively, but it is a far more difficult feat to achieve emotionally! This is the reason many black men feel an estranged resentment towards black women, although they have no alternative but to live with and try to love them.

The human ego is, in large part, a reflection of (or an internalization of) what happens when one person encounters another person. This is especially true when the encounter involves individuals of the opposite sex. Before Grandmother whipped me, a girl was just a girl. After the beating, all females took on a meaning beyond their sex, a meaning symbolized and defined by the color of their skins. And this meaning, this symbolization of pigment severely altered my developing concept of myself as a black boy—a black man—in a world of black and white creatures called women. Although I did not understand the ethics of southern Jim Crow, I adhered to them. As long as I attended that school I walked out of my way to avoid my white friend, and I have never seen her again. But in the dream world, in the world of fantasy and nightmare, I saw her—and have seen her—countless times. And this—the autistic, or vicarious, compensation for the injury one suffers in real life—does not make for therapy, but adds to the diseased way in which the black male conceives of himself, of white women, and of black women too.

For reasons I consider irrelevant here, I have always wanted a sister. The rest is not irrelevant. Shortly after my first "lesson" in Jim Crow, I began to dream that I had a sister. Sometimes my sister would be black. Most of the time she would be white—and even the black sister would be of such light skin that if she wanted to (or if *I* wanted her to) she could pass for white. In both cases, one of the functions of my imaginary sister was to introduce me to imaginary interracial couples. My sister was beautiful, you see, and, of course, not prejudiced. Most of all, she *loved* me. We, my sister, and our interracial friends would do all kinds of things that young people ordinarily do. We played, went to movies, went on bus outings, and so on. We would even fight, but only to make up and become greater comrades. When I say I had such dreams, I do not mean dreaming merely while asleep, I mean daydreaming, outright childhood fantasizing. I made the world *good*; I made black and white people—especially men and women—like and enjoy each other. And yet, there was always the "outside world," a hostile world of blacks and whites of whom we —I, my sister, and friends—had to be cautious. For instance, I fantasized a fabulous apartment left to us by our parents *(you see, our parents were dead)*. And this was where we spent most of our time, hidden from the outside world. When *we* went somewhere in public, we acted in such a way that people could not really tell that we were together. Frequently my dreams assumed a deeper, perhaps more psychiatric, dimension. I would, with her consent, have sex with my sister, the black one. And always she would turn into the white sister. I would begin to scream and run, thinking she was going to yell and bring down the white community on me and my grandmother. But she never did; instead, she would hold me and reassure me that no one would ever know. I always woke up in a cold sweat.

These dreams and fantasies persisted on an ever widening and deepening level throughout my teens—that is, until I finished high school. At that time I began to date rather seriously. My dates were always light-skinned black girls, never dark or *black* ones, no matter how pretty they might have been. For, I know now, my desire for a girl was affected by the myth and taboo of the white woman. I know now why I enjoyed the envy of other black boys—because I had a light-skinned girl friend. As we walked the streets, all eyes, black and white, would linger or flash quickly upon us. And I was proud. But not proud enough. I felt a partial fulfillment of my ego as a black boy, but it was only partial—because although my girl was very light with long black hair, she was still a Negro. She was, for that alone, not as good as a real white girl. I made up for this also by dreaming. Often while we sat cheek to cheek in the dark of a movie, I would look at her through the depraved eye of my mind and imagine her as white—and sometimes I would even grow afraid to touch her face. At about that time the black press had made big headlines of an event in Georgia: a black man had failed to help a desperate white woman escape from the flaming wreckage of an automobile, because he had been afraid of the consequences of laying his black hands on her flesh in order to pull her free. The woman had perished.

To every black boy who grows up in the South, the light-skinned black woman—the "high yellow," the mulatto—incites awe. The white woman incites *more* awe. As a boy I was, to say the least, confused. As I grew

65

older, the desire to see what it was that made white women so dear and angelic became a secret, grotesque burden to my psyche. It is that to almost all black men, no matter how successfully they hide and deny it. And for these reasons—the absurd idolization of the white woman and the equal absurdity of the taboo surrounding her—there arises within almost all blacks a sociosexually induced predisposition for white women. The fact that few blacks will readily admit this is due more to their knowledge that black women and whites in general bitterly disapprove of it, than to their honesty. For if a situation occurs where a white woman makes herself accessible to a black man, the black man usually takes her. However cautiously, he takes her at once like a grateful baby and like a savage monster. He suffers mixed emotions of triumph, fulfillment, and guilt. At eighteen I had an affair with a white girl in a small town in Alabama. She met me one night in an abandoned railroad yard. I was nervous and scared, not primarily that someone might discover us—although I was scared of that too— but mainly just because she was *white*. I kissed her mouth. I wanted to see if it was different, if it was better than a black mouth. I looked at her for the first time directly and long. It felt like magic—and yet why? Why! I was baffled over whatever white women were supposed to possess that made them objects of grave consequences. Why were they so important? I wondered about her anatomy. I ran my hands over her body. I wanted to know if it was different, if it felt better than black flesh. I kept wanting to find out what made white womanhood *white womanhood*; I wanted to unearth the quality that made her angelic and forbidden.

My search failed. There was nothing objectively or inherently emotional that was *that* different or angelic. Yet there was something—and it was distorted and horrible. There was all of the southern ideology of racism and sex that had been instilled in my mind, in my very skin, and no doubt in hers too. Cautiously, diligently, maddeningly I took her. I hated her for what she made me feel, for the good and bad that she inspired in me; for what she *reduced* me to. I loved her too! But somehow I could not purge myself of the feeling that it was wrong and perverse. I came away not knowing whether I felt elated or outraged.

When I was a student at a southern black college, one of the unexpected experiences I had was when I went to the library one day and pulled from the shelves a book which contained a collection of writings by African-Americans. I opened the book and there on the first page was the title in large caps: *WHAT THE NEGRO WANTS*. Just below the title something had been scribbled and erased. But I could still discern what it had been; it was a "reply" to the title of the book, *WHAT THE NEGRO WANTS:* "Some white *p- - -y.*"

The southern white man claims that black men are possessed by a savage urge to have sex with white women, or, more correctly, that black men want to rape white women. If there is truth in this claim, it is not because of any natural urge in the black man. The desire to have sex with or to rape the white woman is a by-product of what racism, Jim Crow, and prejudice have made of not only the black man but everybody affected by American bigotry.

In the mind and the life of the black man the white woman symbolizes at once his freedom and his bondage. She is made into an object of temptation and repulsion, love and hate. It appears to me that the black man's sexual existence in the South is predicated upon the existence of the white woman who is inaccessible. A kind of reverse racism sets in. The black man, like everyone else, hates what he cannot love; he wants what he cannot have; he degrades and mutilates that which humiliates and deranges him.

"Just look at all those proud, white asses shaking like jelly," said a friend of mine as we drove through the downtown section of Nashville, Tennessee. "I hate those white ugly bitches," he went on. "They think they own the world. And they do. Say, look at that one. What a fine dish! I'd like to rape her with a telegraph pole." He laughed. "No I wouldn't either. I'd use my own penis. Look at them, coming out of those offices, sitting on their fine asses all day, doing nothing. I could screw every one I see. Especially that one over there in the blue skirt. I bet I could make her moan and groan like no white man's ever done, make her *love* me. Damn!—the white man's got everything—money, jobs, even our own women—everything! And don't know what to do with any of it. Say, what you smiling at? What you thinking?" "Nothing," I lied. I was studying his face, the way it grew tight, tense, the way it lit up or flickered as he talked. There was hatred, envy, love, fear, impotence, desire, and the mixture of emotions that almost every black male learns to feel towards the white woman. I was thinking, Could this man actually commit rape? Was it possible that the white woman could have such an effect upon an otherwise bright and well-bred black man?

I had known him for several years. We had come through college together at the head of our class. Another year in graduate school and he would be a chemist. He had already been offered a top position with a major chemical firm. I was pondering the nature of a way of life that could cripple a healthy individual to the point that the individual, black or white, could lose control and, if the situation occurred, become a rapist, heaving and ravishing like a wild animal. I am well aware that, like murder, rape has many motives. But when the motive for rape, however psychotic, is basically racial, that is a different matter. I think now that, at one time or another, in every black man who grows up in the South, there is a rapist, no matter how hidden. And that rapist has been conceived in the black man by a system of morals based on guilt, hatred, and human denial.

My friend, the chemist, as far as I know, never raped a white woman. He did something better than that, or maybe worse. He married and divorced, and then remarried. His second marriage took place in California, to a white woman from Texas.

Not only are the customs, attitudes, and sentiments in America unequivocally against personal relationships between black men and white women, but the taboos against such relations are incorporated in the legal statutes of southern cities and states. In addition to this, the mere association of black men and white women in any manner whatever, except in the strictest formal or business sense, is a crime. In Selma, Alabama, for instance, a black man can be arrested simply for talking to ("social-izing with") a white woman in private or public sur-roundings. This means, as interpreted by local police, that a black man can be jailed for walking too close to a white woman on the sidewalk!

In the North, unlike the South, there are very few laws prohibiting interracial relations between the sexes. It is not the law, then, that is being tested when an inter-racial couple marries or is seen on the streets north of the Mason-Dixon Line. What are being tested are the informal attitudes and disapprovals. It is axiomatic that the sentiments of an overwhelming majority of northern whites are against interracial couples, especially couples comprising black men and white women. More signifi-cant are the deeply embedded emotions of the black man himself toward white women.

There is much truth in the adage that it is a relatively easy matter to take the boy out of the country, but one does not so easily take the country out of the boy. Those blacks who have come from the South, but who still have the South in them, react in the North to the white woman in more or less the same pattern that they learned in the South. They may work beside and indulge in conversation with white women, but it is all on the up and up, strictly impersonal. By and large, one hears and sees in action in the North the same attitude of ambiva-lence and avoidance toward the white woman as one sees and hears in the South. This is especially true with older black people. Then, too, most blacks in the North live, for one bad reason or another, in ghettos. They may work outside of the ghetto in an "integrated atmo-sphere," but they *live* in milieus that are difficult to distinguish from the ones in which black people live in the South. Not only does the "outer society" punish a black man for associating with a white woman, his very own people extract an oath from him to associate exclusively with his own kind. The greatest pressure of this sort comes, understandably, from the black female, who feels that her chances of obtaining a man are lessened when she has to compete not only with females of her own race but with white women too.

At present, an African-American who marries or embarks on a personal relationship with a member of the white race, is ostracized and intimidated by such groups as the Black Nationalists and the Black Muslims. Basically, these groups, fanatic in zeal, employ in reverse the same arguments against race mixing as their white counterparts who are racists. They extol the "purity" of black womanhood, exalt the "superiority" of black people, and insist on thoroughly living up to the creed which says: "Buy Black, Think Black," and most of all, "Love Black!" During the Birmingham rallies that took place in Harlem, Eartha Kitt was booed and jeered off the rostrum by hundreds of blacks because, among other things, she had married a white man. A brilliant young black man was fired from his position with a now defunct organization because his wife, whose dedication to the African-American struggle is outmatched only by her beauty, is white. Pressure is also put on African-Americans to love and marry black by a class of blacks who otherwise go along with the integration and equality program. These blacks claim that, since the sex issue is so explosive, and the segregationists use this issue to their advantage, black men should avoid intimacy with white women because it will "hurt the movement for civil rights." Always, the strongest pressure, on the part of both black and white, is not so much against Negro women marrying white men as against black men marrying white women.

Now, while I recognize the existence of these pressures from both the white and black communities in the North, I must give credence to the proposition that in the mind of the black man, the North constitutes the proving ground of his freedom. Coming North has always been, and still is, an experience of intense anticipation for the African-American. Among all of the things the black man looks forward to, encountering the white woman is definitely one of them. I recall when I was a youth living in the South, a certain young man went North. Upon his return all of the boys from the neighborhood gathered around him. Among the most important questions we asked was, "Did you meet any white girls, did you see any blacks with white women? Are things really like they say they are up North?" When the young man, with obvious pride, pulled from his wallet a photograph of a beautiful white girl, we all sighed, and a great loneliness settled over us.

In matters such as housing, employment, civil rights, and so forth, the African-American in the North takes a positive position, even if he is disillusioned in the end. More often than not, he is. But in the presence of the white woman he is not so sure of himself. He has heard stories about white women and black men in the North from (as indicated above) blacks who came North and returned South. He realizes that bits of truth and bits of fantasy are interwoven in such tales. Because of the tre-

72

mendous fear and trembling that has been shot into his brain while living in the South, the black man, even in the North, cannot completely extricate himself from the cataclysm of emotions he has learned to feel toward the white woman. In her presence, he is in a quandary: Should he act like most blacks, as if he were still down South? Should he be forthright but businesslike? Should he approach her in all his manliness as he would any other woman? Or should he strive for some kind of equilibrium or compromise between these attitudes? At first he does not know.

I recall when I first came North I got along fine. I sat anywhere I chose, ate anywhere, looked for a job anywhere. In all of this, however, I dreaded the white woman. I pretended otherwise, but I know now that I did. The first time a white woman sat down beside me on the subway, it was difficult for me to control myself. I stole glances at her out of the corner of my eye. I looked at others on the subway to check their reaction. I could smell her perfume, and I was relieved when she got off. I also remember making the rounds of employment agencies. Whenever the interviewer was a white female, I grew tense and my hands perspired. On one occasion I made the interview short and hurried out of the office. The young woman who was interviewing me appeared tender and fragile, yet she treated me as if I—the *real* I— did not exist. I was not ashamed of being a black man, and I wanted her to recognize me as such and not treat me like some anonymous entity. I could tell she was conscious of my blackness, while deliberately pretending she was not. I do not want anybody to love me simply because I am black. Neither do I want people to ignore me because of my color.

It seems to me that every black male who encounters a white woman in the North is subtly testing the degree to which he is accepted by the way the woman reacts toward the visual perception of his person as a black man. Much of this is due to plain curiosity. A sort of flirtation with the unknown, a desire for new experience, or simply a desire for a fuller, if not richer, life. And when, as is so often the case, the black person is not accepted, he reverts back to the southern ethics of race relations. He rejects the white woman, he hates that which denies his existence, he stays his social and psychological distance, and he spouts the rhetoric of sour grapes.

On the other hand, one does not walk the streets of any major northern city without passing a few mixed couples here and there. For one reason or another, the various external pressures and overt social taboos are not severe enough in the North to prevent some black men from pursuing the white woman. In fact, it may be these very pressures and taboos that stimulate the black man to pursue the white woman. Emphasizing the perils and sacrifices of associating with a white woman may tend to enhance her value in the eyes of the black man. To such a black man, the prize is worth the challenge. Indeed, it is this sort of spirit or "guts" that has made America a great nation. The rugged individualist, the man who transcends the chains of background and provincialism to surge ahead toward new frontiers is an American hero. For the contemporary black man the white woman definitely represents a "new frontier."

In all "civilized" societies there seems to be something

about men and women so that, from time to time, one finds various couples from diverse backgrounds falling in love and marrying, despite the taboos that may exist against these unions. I suspect, or at least hope, the same principle applies to some interracial love affairs and marriages.

However, I do not think that the personality forces that mobilize most blacks who seek relations with white women are free of ulterior or psychiatric motives. I have in mind those blacks, mostly youths, who journey from Harlem down to Greenwich Village every weekend with one purpose in mind—to "make some ofay chick." The Lower East Side of New York (the "East Village") is notorious for its interracial, bohemian-type weekend parties. White girls make themselves readily available to black boys, and black boys shuffle through the assortment of white flesh like fierce hunters on safari. As one goes from party to party, from one beatnik bar to the other, one becomes aware of a kind of mutual conspiracy between white women and black men. One of the features that characterizes the behavior of these blacks is their attempt to intimidate the white male by making free play with his woman. At one of these parties I observed such a scene in action. There was a young, sandy-headed, timid-looking fellow standing in one corner of the room. On his arm was a shapely girl of about nineteen. A tall, black, mawkish but rather handsome man emerged in the center of the room. He was pretending to be drunker than he really was. He reeled and tottered, peered around. I watched him. Then he saw the couple. He staggered over to them, reached for the girl, caught her hand and muttered, "Le's do the thang." The girl followed him onto the floor and he danced her a vulgar whirl, no, *twirl* is the right word. He fondled her buttocks and breasts right there on the floor, and mumbled words into her mouth. All the while he was glancing over her head at the sandy-haired fellow in the corner, who was fuming but trying his best to ignore the scene. When the black man had finished, he slapped the girl on her round, plump buttocks. Then he went over to the fellow in the corner and, with a smirk on his mouth, said, "Thank you, dad." It cut like a razor.

I know for certain—and I *must* say this—that white men in the North show more restraint and courtesy in their dealings with black women. Not once have I seen a white man insult or intimidate his black girl in mixed company. Maybe he is afraid, or perhaps he has no need for it.

In the confines of the hip, the beatniks, and the young liberals one learns that many blacks exploit the exploitable. In the process, the blacks exploit themselves. They parade and display their Negroness. No, no, it is the *nigger* in them that they display, the stereotype to which white women must respond in order to prove their liberalness or hiptitude. For these black men, "making the ofay chick" is at once an act of aggression against white society and against the girl herself.

In this connection it is well to mention a term that, with the rise of African nationalism, has become more and more a part of the black man's vocabulary. The word is "negritude." From what I understand, this word is supposed to lend pride and even superiority to Negro characteristics, both physical and cultural, as opposed to the devaluation of these characteristics by the standards of the white world. While there is much validity to negritude, I suspect that many, too many, black men use negritude to exploit white women. In fact, this is their only appeal. Many such men, for instance, will not comb their hair or take a bath, and they exaggerate their Negroness in order to obtain a white girl. And it is true that many white girls, who are trying so desperately to liberate themselves from prejudice and racial bias, respond, however painful it may be to do so, to this type of "negritude," this kind of vulgarization of the so-called "black mystique."

I think of a story told to me by a young black man who had just moved into a new neighborhood. He inquired, among the blacks who had been in the neighborhood for some time, as to the availability of girls. One black man told him,

Look man, you don't have to worry about getting a chick. You are *black*; all you have to do is walk into a party and act *black*, act mean . . .

A great many of these black men hate white women, and having sexual relations with them is one way of destroying or mutilating the enemy (ofay).

Surprisingly (or is it to be expected?), there are men who are afflicted with the white man's mythological concept of Negro sexhood. Their behavior around white women is strictly sexual. They prance around, jump up and down, gyrate their pelvises, and nearly every word they speak has a sexual reference. It is not simply a matter of trying to exploit the white man's sex image of the black man. No! Such men would have us believe that they live entirely in their sex, and, like raving cripples, they do! These *Negroes* are *diseased* by the racist's grotesque sex image of them, which, after all, is nothing more than a myth. It is not uncommon to discover that many of the men who constantly strive to project such mammoth sexuality around white women are lonely men. In fact, they are sexual failures with black women, if not repressed homosexuals. At the bottom of their hearts many of the black men who pursue or marry white women have the same concept of white women as do the white racists. This is understandable, for, *like the white racists, these Negroes are victims of the myth of sacred white womanhood.* For instance, a black writer admitted that his white wife was a "jewel, too lovely and delicate to make love to." The writer keeps his "jewel" in the house and seldom lets her go anywhere. She is his secret "prize." Meanwhile he "runs around" pursuing black women. On the other hand, some black men react in the opposite way—and here I have in mind those men we see daily (in Greenwich Village, for instance) who make a public display of hugging and caressing their white women on the streets, in restaurants, and wherever there are people to watch. "It was my way of defying the society," stated an older black man as he recalled that he used to do the same thing. He further stated:

It was my way of getting back at the white world. Even during intercourse, I was getting back at white folks for everything they inflicted upon me as a Negro. But that kind of thing wears lean after a while—when you get older I mean—and you settle down to love her and forget about the white world; I mean, if you love her in the first place.

78

I might add that, it seems to me, many black men never get over "that kind of thing." None of their relationships with white women ever get over "that kind of thing." None of their relationships with white women ever progress beyond the state of "getting back at the white world" through sadistic treatment of white women. And to my mind, this seems as "sick and disgusting" as the sadistic treatment of Negro women in the South by white racists. And yet one gets the impression, deep behind the smoldering eyes (acting "mean"), that there is an intense desire on the part of many of these men to really love the white woman. But because of the deranged emotional fabric with which racism in America has afflicted the majority of such black men, they are, alas, incapable of genuine love for *any* woman.

Again, in Greenwich Village, as in other parts of the North, one finds also the professional white-woman chaser, or more correctly, the white-woman seducer. Such blacks earn their living—food, clothing, drink, rent —from white women who are starved for attention and affection. The black man is not necessarily handsome; in fact, I think it is better for the woman if he is unattractive, that is, by white standards. For the women who are susceptible to this kind of black man are predominantly depraved women who despise themselves for one reason or another. The professional white-woman seducer is aware of this; he capitalizes on it. He does not love these women. He cannot love them. Like all pimps, the professional hustler of white women is beyond love, for he has come to believe that it is only for fools and babies.

In Baldwin's *Another Country*, the jazz musician, Rufus, who lives with a southern-born, socially defunct white woman, is the fictional image of the extremely paranoid black man who marries or "shacks up" with a white woman. Rufus hated his white girl friend, he hated her very "whiteness." In and through her, he hated the whole society. Coupled with this, Rufus hated himself for being black. On both counts he loved and hated his white girl friend, the symbol of all that was good and evil in his life. Hate, sadistic love, and resentment won out. Rufus not only beat her unmercifully, he committed every atrocity a man can commit against a woman. In the end he drove her insane and himself to suicide.

In too many of the environments where interracial sex is sought, it is the Rufus type of syndrome—the hunger, the hatred, the love and resentment for white women—that one discerns smoldering beneath the eyes of black men. The would-be greats, the jazz musicians, the small-time hipsters, the disgruntled writers, poets, and painters, the marijuana smokers, the seekers of thrills and orgies, the misfits, the socially deformed, the outcasts—all are possessed by a design on the white woman which is chillingly similar to the white racist's design on the black woman. To the black man who is sexually sick, the white woman represents an object for symbolic mutilation as well as an escape from a despised self through the act of sexual intercourse. To the depraved black man, every white woman is the living embodiment of the forces that have oppressed and crippled him.

The history of cults, movements, cultures, and cliques prove one thing, if nothing else. No ideology—political, national, religious, or otherwise—is strong enough to restrict an individual's preference for a certain approved group or class of females. Strangely enough, or perhaps it is altogether natural, young Africans in this country tend to avoid close ties with American Negroes, to snub them with superior airs. It is nothing, on the other hand, for these proud young Africans to date and cater to white women. I am certain that most American blacks—especially the Black Muslims and Black Nationalists—would be shocked to know that the first and perhaps foremost African-American leader, Frederick Douglass, married in 1884 a white woman, Helen Pitts, who was his secretary while he held the post of Recorder of Deeds for the District of Columbia. Blacks were "shocked and disappointed." Everyone, including Douglass's children and his long-trusted house servant, felt betrayed. Of late, a rather accomplished black man of letters has remarked that this marriage was the "most dramatic challenge to color prejudice in America."[1] Any oppressed group, when obtaining power, tends to acquire the females of the group which has been the oppressor.

Although racism of any sort is ideological in content, its effect upon the individual is psychopathic. As Sartre has brilliantly shown (*Portrait of an Anti-Semite*), a man prejudiced against Jews may either burst with pornographic sexual excitement or may become suddenly impotent when confronted by a woman who is Jewish. The same thing applies to both sides of the racial coin in the United States today.

In America, however, where the African-American is the underdog and the white woman is the great symbol of sexual purity and pride, the black man is often driven

[1] See Arna Bontemps, *100 Years of Negro Freedom* (New York: Dodd, Mead & Co., 1961), pp. 111–13.

to pursue her *in lieu of* aggrandizing his lack of self-esteem. Having the white woman, who is the prize of our culture, is a way of triumphing over a society that denies the black man his basic humanity. Going up the color ladder in America is one way of acquiring status. Within the black community, value is distributed on the basis of shades of pigment. A man who marries a light-skinned black woman has "achieved" more prestige through his marriage than one who marries a darker woman. Similarly, for many black men the white woman is the zenith of status symbols.

In one of Langston Hughes's poems, he writes about black babies in Alabama having white mammies who rocked them in their laps and nestled them close to their white breasts. There is straight psychoanalytical truth in his words. It seems altogether plausible that deep in the psyches of many blacks there is the rejection of their black mothers, or, positively stated, there is the wish for a white mother. After all, if the black man had a white mother, the chances are he would not be black. If the white racist has an incestuous urge for black women because of the infantile or boyhood memory of his black mammy who nursed and suckled him on her big, black breasts, I think it is reasonable to explore the possibility of some black men relating to white women on the same principle.

I know black men whose relationship with their white women approximates this type of situation. It is always embarrassing to visit their homes. The black man is usually a steady drinker, he does very little around the apartment, he "writes" or engages in some other "artistic endeavor," but he very seldom produces. To show how unprejudiced he is, he never fails to bring up the race problem. He lies all over and fondles his wife deliberately in your presence. One thing is certain—without her he is nothing. Unless she needs this kind of neurotic behavior, the wife or lover has a very hard time with this type of black man. Even if the woman is neurotic herself, sometimes the situation becomes so absurd and embarrassing that she will order her black husband to stop and sit down in an individual chair. On one occasion, a young woman burst into tears in my presence.

Some black men who seek out white women show a marked readiness for jealousy when they see a white man with a black woman (one of "ours"). They will try to intimidate the woman by making some kind of "smart" remark or by accusing her of "selling out the race." One black girl informed me that it is very common for a black man, upon finding out that she is married to a white fellow, to walk up to her and whisper in her ear, "Are you being satisfied?" Such black men act and talk like schizophrenics. They preach "black pride" and exhibit "black jealousy," on the one hand, while on the other hand, they are constantly haunting interracial bars, parties, and so forth, always seeking to woo the white woman. They are afflicted with what I have termed elsewhere "the syndrome of blackness." Despising both races, they want to be white and black at the same time. They want to eat their color and have it too.[2]

With black men who *have* to marry white women, much more than status or an attempt to escape a despised self is involved. There is something metaphysical

[2] See my article, "Black Muslims and White Liberals," *Negro Digest*, October 1963.

about their need for white women. I believe that this was the case with a famous black writer. He was great in his own person. He did not need a white woman to display to the world as a sign of his having "achieved." He needed—I mean *needed*—a white woman for something more urgent than this. Elsewhere I have written that, in the disposition of the deformed, there is the organic craving to be loved by those who have crippled them, to be redeemed by those who have damned them. The hero of Richard Wright's second major novel, *The Outsider*, is a young black man named Cross Damon. In the course of the book he murders four people. Cross is a clever, intellectual, superbly self-controlled man, and no one can accuse him of the crimes. Although dread and guilt weigh heavily upon him, throughout the entire novel he never breaks down—except once. The occasion involves a white woman:

"Have mercy on me," we hear Cross cry out to her, "Pity me; be my judge; tell me if I am to live or die."

He is on his knees, and he begs the white woman to *judge* him, to absolve him from his sins, from the guilt that floods his being. The woman sympathizes, but she really does not know what her black prince is talking about.

Because the black man is hated, South and North, so deeply on the basis of his blackness, any black man who receives kind treatment from a white person is indeed grateful—and especially so if the white person is a female. After the depraved self-concept that centuries of racism has wrought within the African-American, a simple act of human kindness from a white female elicits the

84

most extreme feelings of gratitude from the black man. He wants to respond in the most tender way possible—sexually. Even a white man, John Griffin, who had dyed his skin and was pretending to be a black man, felt gratitude when a southern white woman merely refrained from staring at him in the usual hateful manner. He writes:

She merely looked at me and did not change her expression. My gratitude to her was so great it astonished me![3]

A very dark black man who served as an informant for this book reported how he felt when he first experienced a white woman who said she loved him because he was black.

Man, I felt like a king. And yet I felt humble like a baby. I didn't let her know it though. But hell, man, nobody has ever loved me because I was black—not even my own wife. It was the first time in my whole life that anybody ever made me feel proud of being black.

Precisely! Many black men who are black, and therefore "ugly" (by white standards), find it difficult to acquire a suitable black mate. Black women tend to choose black men on one of two bases: 1) the black man must *not* be "black and ugly"; or 2), if he is, he must then be a professional man such as a doctor, lawyer, or professor. A "black and ugly" man, if he is not rich or a professional, usually has to settle for any female he can get and from any sort of background. Even if he is a professional and succeeds in getting a woman who is educated and more or less refined in manners and social outlook, her

[3] John Griffin, *Black Like Me* (New York: Signet Books, 1963), p. 117.

resentment for his blackness comes out sporadically, if not constantly, to plague his ego. For instance, one black man who fits the above description reported the following about his "light-skinned," educated wife.

I see her sometimes looking at me when I am naked or just when I am milling around the house—I see the resentment in her well-guarded eyes. Whenever I do something she doesn't like, she always calls me a black bastard. If she catches me in a lie, I'm not a lying bastard, I'm a *black* bastard. If I cheat on her, I'm not a cheating bastard, I'm a *black* bastard. No matter what it is she's mad at me about, I'm always a black bastard.

Anyone who is familiar with what happens between dark-skinned black men and women when they are arguing can bear witness to the racial epithets that the couple fling back and forth at one another. "Black bastard," "thick-lip bastard," "ugly nigger," "nappy-head bitch," "black dog," and so on. Such epithets, no matter how they are used, do considerable damage to the black's appreciation of himself. African-American have come to think of themselves in terms of white standards of beauty and attractiveness. This is what someone has called *the mark of oppression*. The point is, however, that many of the darker black men who pursue white mates do so because their own women have rejected them because they are "black and ugly." Whereas, white women, not having actually suffered the negative valuation accorded Negroid features, can live with a so-called "black and ugly" black man without constantly making the black man secretly despise himself for the way he happens to look. Because the white woman is not herself involved with all the ego effects of being black, it is even possible for her to look, if she will, at the black man with fresh eyes and see him as some kind of "exotic beauty," which the black woman who is involved with being black herself cannot do. Thus, we hear some black men proclaiming that such and such a white woman treats them better than the females of their own race. (Needless to say, all of this applies to black women and white men also.)

Although the African-American will quickly deny the assertion that he has a religious urge for the white woman, in a great number of instances the black man not only seeks aggression in taking the white woman's body, but through her flesh he renders himself up as if to God, praying that his sense of guilt for his blackness will be conjured away. For this kind of black man, sex with the white woman is an exigency as holy as Communion. It is a matter of sin and absolution.

I have stated that the whole denial of the black man's humanity, specifically his masculinity, is in large measure predicated upon the existence of the white world. The white world is virtuous, holy, chaste. The black world is dirty, savage, sinful. At the center of the clean world stands the white woman. To blacks who feel and suffer the atrocities of racism and inhumanity with intensity, one of the necessary components for transcending or "cleansing" the sin of blackness from their beings is to possess the white woman. According to the myth of white supremacy, it is the white woman who is the "Immaculate Conception" of our civilization. Her body is a holy sacrament, her possession is a sort of ontological affirmation of the black man's being. Hatred, guilt, bitterness, love, and resentment are all involved, I suspect. But with men like Richard Wright, the magnitude of their commitment to truth and life—rather than to death and hate—makes their love and comradeship burn through. Few white women marry black men of this caliber. Those who do should count themselves among the fortunate.

FOUR

The White Man

I was fifteen years old. I was standing on a corner in the downtown section of Atlanta, Georgia. I was waiting for the bus. I saw a man approaching me. He was white, and was shabbily dressed; he seemed somewhat intoxicated. Yes—as he spoke I smelled the odor of alcohol on his breath. He wanted information. This is what he said: "Boy, can you tell me where I can get some Negra p - - - y." I stepped back and looked at him. His face was red, without any signs of embarrassment, he stared me straight in my eyes. A hot sensation shot throughout my body. I wanted to give him a piece of my mind! But I am black and he is white, and I know better. Silently, I contained my indignation and boarded the bus.

Several years later. I was a full-grown man, coming out of a restaurant on 125th Street, Harlem, New York. The sun was setting. The streets were crowded with people. It was Friday night. I lit a cigarette and started walking towards the subway. A man stepped in line with my pace, which was very casual. I glanced at the man. He was looking at me. He was well-dressed, with tie, suit, and shined shoes. He had the appearance of a businessman or a politician—except for his eyes, which seemed to hold some dark secret, something in them that made me wonder . . . maybe this man was a homosexual. As he stepped closer to me and took hold of my arm, I was certain of it. "Excuse me," he said, "would you know where I can find a colored woman, a nice one!" And he winked. I looked directly into his white face. I was not angered, no, I was surprised, shocked. A feeling of superiority came over me. I laughed. I told him yes, and pointed in the direction of a notorious bar. The man seemed happy; he strode off towards his destination, his fate.

I refuse to believe that I simply *look* like a procurer of black women for white men. Besides, other black men— most black men—have had the same experience. The fact that a white man can approach any black person, a total stranger, about a matter as intimate as sex with a black woman reflects that man's poverty of respect for the black male and female, and is also an index to the nature of the man's own sexual morality. Few blacks would dare ask a white friend, let alone a total stranger, where they could find a white woman to sleep with. Moreover, if I, for instance, found myself possessed by an urge for a white woman, she would have to be something other than a slut or a prostitute.

Specifically, the white supremacist's (or racist's) concept of the black female is that all of them are sluts and prostitutes; at best, they are objects of open sexual lust. In the mind of the racist, the northern ghettos are viewed as jungles of smoldering black flesh against which the prejudiced white man can act out his lewd concept of the sex act. Certainly racism in America has affected the sexual morality of both races towards one another. But it seems to me that it is the white man, the white racist, who exemplifies the more pornographic emotions when he thinks of or actually sees a black female. To the majority of white men the mere thought of sexual relations with a black woman is either pruriently disgusting or obscenely exciting.

The very anatomy (legs, breasts, buttocks) of the black woman is viewed in one or both of the above ways. As one walks the streets of any northern city one cannot help noticing the way white men leer, with lewd intimacy, at the bodies of black women. In the garment district of New York, for instance, where hundreds of black and Puerto Rican women work, during the noon lunch hour the sidewalks are packed with white men from all areas of life, in various stages of youth and age. Some are obviously well-to-do men, executives with wives and families securely tucked away in suburban homes. All, whoever they are, mill around on street corners—their eyes and mouths reveal a lascivious desire for every black and Puerto Rican woman who passes. It is a daily marathon. No doubt some of the women secretly appreciate the fact that they are getting attention from and can arouse desire in these men. But the quality of this desire is similar to that which is aroused in a man who is sexually excited by the sight of, say, dogs in coitus.

Down South, where racism is rampant, a common experience of all black males is the humiliation of hearing about and often witnessing black women being fondled, insulted, and seduced by white men. A black youth who lives in Georgia relates the following:

> The insurance man brushes up against Mama when he talks to her. He comes to our house two times a month, and he does this. I see him. Sometimes he touches her with his hands. I see him do it. My mama knows he do it too. But she don't ever say anything. She just smiles. When he goes she calls him a dog.

Several years ago in a southern town which is famous for bombings, there occurred an incident in which the police took a black girl right off the street and away from her black escort and put her into their patrol car. They drove to the outskirts of the city and raped her in open daylight. Few such incidents are reported in the news, and, contrary to what one might think, this is indicative of the frequency with which they occur. In the same city, in 1960, a group of college students who were touring the city reported the following incident:

> Well . . . we were all walking down the street; I mean, we had come out of the motel and were on our way to the stadium where the game [football] was being played. Suddenly we heard a woman scream. We all looked and she was across

the street, and a drunk white man had run his hand under her dress. When she screamed, the police, who were down on the corner, heard her like we did, and they drove up there fast. Well, they arrested the man. But what happened was, when we got around the corner, we saw the same policemen letting the man go. And they were all laughing.

In large measure, it is the police in the South who, when they do not commit such acts themselves, allow or actually encourage the intimidation of black women by white men. The black woman in the South has had no rights (and to some extent still has none) that white men were or are obliged to respect. It was common knowledge in the southern neighborhood where I grew up that the police who Gestapo-ed the vicinity were having affairs with many of the women, married and single. One day a black man surprised a policeman with his wife and killed the officer. A great hush fell over the community. Despite the fact that the officer was shot with his own revolver, while he was literally trying to put on his pants, the black man was convicted and sentenced to life in prison.

Often when a black woman is arrested in the South, she is made to strip in front of the police, or whipped in the nude, or actually raped. During the heyday of the freedom rides, a few reports of this sort leaked out and were printed in the northern press. Many of the young women who made those rides were subjected to this kind of humiliation. Indeed, almost every black woman who works where there are white men must, at some point or another, encounter sexual insults. This is especially true in the area of domestic service, where the black maid, or cook, or what-have-you is virtually at the mercy of the man of the house, since he can threaten her with dismissal or entice her with personal favors and monetary rewards.

The late Richard Wright wrote a story, "Man of All Work," in which he tells of a black man who, because his wife was ill and he could not find a man's job, dressed up as a woman and answered an ad for a maid. The black man succeeded in his disguise until the man of the house came home intoxicated one day and made some rather persistent advances, whereupon he discovered that his "maid" could throw quite a punch and was far stronger than he was. Then, of course, the whole scheme was exposed. In key cities of the South in such states as Louisiana, Alabama, South Carolina, Florida, and Georgia, mulattoes constitute a large proportion of the black population. Mississippi, where segregation is said to be strictest, has the highest number of "high yellows." Where did all of these "white" (light-skinned) blacks come from if the racial lines are as thoroughly drawn as whites in these states insist they are?

In the South, where the entire black community has been an object of pillage and harassment, the intimacies of black women have constituted the main prize. The ethics of Jim Crow have given the white man relatively free access to the black man's woman. Certainly, strict taboos against race mixing are enforced and maintained; but the enforcement is *one way*. The African-American is segregated in theory and in fact; the white man is segregated only in theory. This type of unequal relationship has an historical basis, stretching back to slavery.

During the era of slavery, white women were inaccessible to black men. On the other hand, all black women were accessible to white men. During this period the white man had as much sex with the black women of his plantation as he did with his wife. Sometimes more. Lillian Smith, a white woman who was brought up in the South and is thoroughly familiar with its history, tradition, and secrets, writes:

In the white southern woman's dictionary *Discrimination* could be defined as a painful way of life which too often left an empty place in her bed and an ache in the heart.[1]

Because his concept of the sex act made him think of it as something dirty, sinful, and savage, the white Southerner found it difficult to relate to his own women. He was inhibited by the Calvinist interpretation of sex as befouling the dignity of man. He therefore cringed from his manly duties towards his wife, and if he did make love to her, the act was marred by his guilt and shame. No doubt, as Lillian Smith has indicated, white women suffered. The white man raised or lowered his women to the status of sexless dolls and genteel ladies. The myth of "white womanhood" became an integral facet of southern culture.

The white supremacist in the ante-bellum South went into the fields, into ghettos and "nigger" shantytowns. He slept with the servants who kept his house and cooked his food. He was able to do this, or at least he did it, first of all because black women as slaves were defenseless. Secondly, and most important, he did it because he felt that black women were not human beings.

[1] Lillian Smith, *Killers of the Dream* (Garden City, New York: Doubleday Anchor Books, 1963), p. 125.

Black women were animals, outside of the providence of God. The black woman was a "Negress," to whom one could do anything without fear of reprisal from God or conscience. In order to commit an act one conceives of as degrading and sinful, one must find an object one considers degraded and iniquitous. In the minds of the majority of white men during the era of slavery the black woman satisfied these conditions. The modern white supremacists are little different from their slaveholding ancestors.

To some degree, however microscopic, all white men in America, save a few, carry in their perception of black females a dark sexual urge that borders on the vulgar. The lewd concept of Negro sexhood is not exclusively a personal attitude. It is a part of the American ideology towards blacks in general. Few whites, no matter how liberal or unprejudiced they may be, can escape it. For instance, among the whites I interviewed for this book, there was a young New Yorker who spoke of the sexual excitement he felt when in the presence of black women. "I get goose pimples," he said. "There are three [black women] in my office. When I look at them moving about or when I get close . . . They make me uncomfortable. Of course, I don't let on. I act natural . . . I steal glances at them when no one is watching, and I catch myself wanting them. The same thing happens on the street or in the subway, or anywhere. . . . I feel torn and hot inside. Don't get me wrong, I'm no freak . . . I get along fine with women of my own race. Maybe it's because I've never been intimate with a Negro. But . . . they make me feel like . . . when you are a kid and you lock the bathroom door and look at dirty pictures. . . ."

The aberrant or pornographic urge also applies, as we have seen, to the black man's sexual emotions toward the white woman. For the African-American is rarely more than a product of, or at best an adaptation to, American values, racism included. Witness the following:

I know white women ain't better than black ones. I've had both. Fact of the matter is, black women are more free and relaxed, give you more jelly roll, ha, ha, you know what I mean. But yet and still, white women do something to me that our women do not, even ugly ones. And I want to treat 'em mean . . . even though I want 'em or desire 'em . . . or whatever it is they make me feel—I want everyone I see. . . . But, you know, that's crazy.

The vulgar and frequently sadistic sexual emotions that females of the opposite race arouse in too many American men, both black and white, are the effects of living under a prolonged system of racism and white supremacy. However imperceptibly, we are all tinged.

It is the bigot, however, the out-and-out racist, who conceives of black women *solely* as things of flesh with which, or against which, he can commit the licentious act of intercourse. More than any other American male, the racist is ridden by a subconscious sense of sexual self-loathing which is (and here is the crux) manifested in aggressive and lewd designs on the black female.

"Mongrelization" is the repeated cry of southern racists against extending human rights to black people. Yet, it is obvious that if the races have been or are being "mongrelized," the white man is basically responsible and not the African-American. Especially is this true in the South, specifically in the Deep South (the "Black

Belt"), where historically the larger proportion of blacks have been and still are concentrated.

Early during the period of slavery, light-skinned blacks began to appear in the backyards of the great plantation houses of the South. As more and more of these "mulatto" children began to run around in the backyards, guilt feelings fell upon the white man's conscience. But the white man continued to visit, with increasing frequency, the black cabins. He stayed away more and more from the big house. Then there arose in him the suspicion of his wife left alone back there in the big house. The white man began to suspect his wife of doing exactly what he was doing. Of course, his suspicion was groundless, it was virtually impossible for white women to "slip around" with black men during slavery. But somehow, someway, the white man had to get rid of his feelings of guilt. In jealous panic he projected his own transgression onto his women and onto the black male. A guilt so terrible seized the white man that it is as insane now as it was then—devolutionary guilt. "Mongrelizing," writes Lillian Smith, "is a revealing word with connotations of broken taboos and guilt too terrible to say aloud."[2]

The word "mongrelization" was and is a linguistic expression for the white man's sin. And the use of the word today is an index of the white supremacist's concept *not* of the black man's activity with white women, but of the white man's activity with black women. The proper application of the word is to dogs and other animals. This is precisely the mental image the racist has of black

[2] Smith, op. cit., p. 102.

women. Depending upon the extremity of the racist's sense of sexual guilt, he may find black women sexually repugnant or attractive, but never as human females, only as she-dogs.

Rape and other sexual offenses are supposed to be serious crimes in America. Yet white men in the South daily go unpunished for insulting black women. Rarely are white men convicted of rape, even when there is no doubt that they are guilty of it. Black women and men in the South do not often complain, for they have learned that the practice is for the offender to go free, while the complainer receives the punishment. No white man in the South has ever, to my knowledge, been electrocuted for raping a black girl.

John Griffin, the white reporter who traveled through the South posing as a black man, discovered some very shocking things about the Southerner's concept of the Negro, and about the Southerner's concept of his own sexuality. For instance, repeatedly, thinking that Griffin was black, Southerners showed no signs of restraint in approaching and questioning him about their lewd interpretation of what sex was like with and among blacks. Many Southerners, writes Griffin, ". . . appeared to think that the Negro has done all of those 'special' things they themselves have never dared to do . . . they carry the conversation into the depths of depravity. . . ."[3] Here are a few lines of conversation, for example, from Southerners who talked to Griffin:

Now don't try to kid me. I was not born yesterday. You know you've done such-and-such, just like I have. Hell, it's

[3] John Griffin, *Black Like Me*, (New York: Signet Books, 1963), p. 86.

good that way. Tell me, did you ever get a white woman? . . . There's plenty white women who would like to have a good buck Negro.

I understand Negroes are much more broad-minded about such things. . . . You make more of an art—or maybe hobby —of your sex than we do. . . .

You people don't seem to have the inhibitions we have. . . . I understand Negroes do a lot more things—different kinds of sex than we do. . . .[4]

Griffin states that repeatedly he was asked about the size of black genitalia.

While he was working as a shoeshine boy, white male customers would ask where they could obtain black girls. They had no reticence, no shame at all, since they thought they were addressing a black man. "All of them showed us how they felt about the Negro. The idea that we were people of such low morality that nothing could offend us."[5]

The white man's vulgar concept of and lewd desire for the black is best illustrated by a "notice" Griffin found in a Mississippi bathroom for "colored only." On the wall there were a

. . . list of prices a white man would pay for various ages of Negro girls. The whites frequently walked into colored rest rooms, Scotch-taped these notices to the wall. The man offered his services free to any Negro woman over twenty, offered to pay, in an ascending scale, from two dollars for a nineteen-year-old girl up to seven-fifty for a fourteen-year-old, and more for perversion dates.[6]

[4] Ibid., pp. 86–87.
[5] Ibid., p. 30.
[6] Ibid., p. 81.

That the white racist's *bestial* concept of sexual activity with and between blacks is a reflection of his own sexual and moral depravity, cannot be denied. Witness the carnal abuse of a black child by two white men in the presence of white women companions and their children in Rome, Georgia (reported by the New York *Times*, April 3, 1950). To most Southerners, black people have become equated with the forbidden and deranged part of their nature. Indeed, the African-American represents the dark sexual monstrosity that rages in the racist's concept of himself, which he secretly fears will leap out and destroy him every minute of his life. The African-American is the walking nightmare of the white supremacist's sense of moral inadequacy, an inadequacy which engulfs the whole life of the Southerner, but which the Southerner projects entirely into the sexual area.

A point of clarity is in order. For many of us, especially blacks, the South constitutes a solid wall of Jim Crow and racial injustice. Because of this we tend to think of *every* southern white man as a racist. Generalities are too easy to come by, and for that reason they are often inaccurate. While the South is a land of hatred and prejudice, it would be foolish to assume that all Southerners are racists. If we exclude the fanatic who needs to be institutionalized, a great many southern whites are not pathological Negro haters. They, like black people themselves, are products of their environment. In many instances the average Southerner does not have anything against black people, but he must act as if he hates black people simply because his *environment demands* that he does. Any white man or woman who exhibits an attitude toward black people other than the prescribed one of extreme bigotry, is immediately labeled a "nigger lover" and is subject to all types of reprisals, even bodily harm. The pressures upon whites to conform to the practices of racism are often as severe as those placed upon the African-American. This is especially true when it comes to the area of sex.

Relations between white women and black men are absolutely taboo. However, as I have indicated, the white man can and does have relations with black women. This can even be general knowledge, as long as it is not talked about in public. Yet the white man must conform to a specific ethic which compels him to treat his black woman as an animal who deserves no respect. He can sleep with her discreetly, give her mulatto babies, but in all of this he must never act as if he *loves* her.

There are countless black women who are involved with white men in the South. By "involved," I mean they have had or are having affairs with white men. They "slip around" whenever the circumstances are propitious. Most of these affairs are not lasting relationships. They are incidental, even accidental.

I have before me the notes from interviews I managed to arrange with more than a score of such women. It was not easy to seek them out, and once they were found it was even more difficult to get them to talk. Many of them became suspicious when I revealed my intentions. One woman in South Carolina thought I was a detective in the secret employment of her black boy friend.[7]

[7] The factor which seemed to work in my favor was that during the time I embarked upon these interviews I was, over a period of five years, an instructor of sociology at various Negro colleges in the Deep South. Then, too, I have spent most of my life in the South, and I know it thoroughly, especially

Usually a black woman who has an affair with a white man in the South is an unskilled laborer, a domestic, or a waitress, who meets the man in the course of her employment, and money or some other form of material reward serves as the initial inducement. This is as anyone might expect, for black women who are in the higher social brackets (or who have means of support without working at unskilled jobs) are not put in a position where white men may approach them. The fact is, however, that the vast majority of black women in the South are, if not completely jobless, unskilled or semi-skilled workers. There is relatively constant contact between these women and the white world. The white man is the absolute ruler of that world, and a sort of illicit, vicarious intimacy develops between the white man and the black woman. But, as we shall see later, this intimacy, even when it becomes actual, seldom grows beyond its illicit nature on the part of either the man or the woman, but especially on the part of the man. And I believe it is because of this that every woman I talked to showed signs of shame and trepidation.

When I attended college in Nashville, Tennessee, I worked part-time at a nightclub as a waiter. The kitchen workers—dishwasher, cook, cook's helper—were women. It was a practice of the patrons, when they became "high," and the night was nearing its end, to call the black women from the kitchen and dance with them. This last half-hour of the party constituted what many of the patrons called "Show Time." As the three black

---

the black community. I am not a stranger to its people nor to the subtle, in-group modes of communication among African-Americans.

women emerged from the kitchen onto the dance floor, white men would yell out in devil's glee: "Show Time . . . Show Time . . . Show Time!!!"

The cook was about thirty-five years old and rather fat and bouncy. One of the men would take her and begin to dance. Her large breasts and buttocks would jiggle and quake as she "cut the rug" in the center of the floor. Wild laughter and insinuating comments would erupt from the onlookers. The white women would giggle and purse their mouths in enjoyable embarrassment. The men would push their way forward, their eyes wild. They were having an orgy, a vicarious one, but an orgy nevertheless. Then the cook's helper, who was unattractive, would be pulled onto the floor. The two "couples" —the cook and her white partner and the cook's helper and her partner—would really "upset the joint." Rebel yells, clapping, and obscene innuendoes would fill the club. The women's dresses would fly up above their knees, and the crowd of excited white faces would surge around them. Occasionally I—and I was not the only one—would catch the eye of one or several of the white women glaring at the waiters as we stood there on the fringe of the crowd. The white women wanted to participate too; they wanted to have the vicarious sexual contact and the illicit thrill of dancing with a black boy. And we black boys—I am certain—had reciprocal desires. But it seldom happened—some man would pull the tipsy white woman down in her seat and give her a warning look. Even when, on infrequent occasions, it did happen, neither the waiter nor the white girl could really enjoy it—the bitter stares of every white man there would be upon you.

Finally the dishwasher, a shapely, light-skinned, beautiful black woman of twenty, with long black hair, would be taken onto the floor. Then it was really "Show Time." Her clothes were cheap but they clung tenaciously to the curves of her dancing body. And she could dance! Her partner could too. In fact, I am certain that the man was her "boy friend," because none of the men, except him, would ever touch her. The noise and riot would cease. The dishwasher and her man would dance fast, semifast, then a close-up "slow drag," or what is ethnically known as the "belly rub." Involuntary sighs and whispers of alien ecstasy would suffuse the quietness of the club—but not from the white women. Envy, jealousy, hatred, and repugnant stares would appear on their faces. Many of them would wrinkle up their noses. And when it was over, the big man, the dishwasher's partner, would take a tray and call for contributions. The laughter would be orgasmic. Once I saw him slip the dishwasher a separate bill of her own.

After being fondled and slapped on their buttocks, the black women (especially the dishwasher) would drop their heads and saunter back to the kitchen. When the place was empty, the women never failed to express their disgust over what had happened. They knew that they were being used as vicarious sex toys, as "Negresses," and not as human females. They "hated" white men; but what could they do? They needed the money, and it was a white man's world even if they did not approve of it.

I met a black woman who was a schoolteacher in Georgia. At the time I interviewed her she was on the edge of a nervous breakdown because, as she put it, she detested the manner in which the affair she was having had to be conducted. Over a period of time she had fallen in love with the man, but in her estimation it was "hopeless."

"How did you meet him?"

"At an interracial meeting, almost a year ago."

"Interracial meeting in Georgia!"

"Yes. Georgia isn't as bad as some of you Northerners think—at least, not this city."

"I'm not a Northerner. I was born in the South, educated down here, and I've worked all over the South. Go ahead, please."

"It was during the sit-ins—one of the first times whites and blacks had come together for the purpose of trying to work out plans for—what do they call it?— 'more harmonious relations between the races.' That night, the night of the meeting, I was impressed with what F. [the white man in question] had to say. He was the most liberal there. Oh, he's no radical—who is? But he is honest and has integrity. He doesn't talk out of both sides of his mouth like a lot of southern would-be liberals."

"How does he look?"

She sipped coffee, eyed me, smiled. "He's tall, handsome, attractive. And he went to a northern university. If that's what you want to know."

"Go right ahead."

"Well, I guess I let him know I liked him. Men can tell those things. I liked his views. He liked me too. From time to time, he seemed to be talking directly to me and not to anyone else there. When the meeting was over, we all, everybody, went to a restaurant. You know, in the colored part of town, and had coffee. Well, he sat with me, next to me, and we talked, just talked, mostly small talk to each other when we were not paying attention to what the others were talking about. To make it short, we arranged to meet, alone—"

"Where? How did you work it? Did you meet at your house?"

"The first time I drove—I have a car, you see—we met in our cars out on the new highway they were building at the time. And we saw each other like this a lot of times. There's a hotel here too you know, we've gone there several times; that is, one at a time. I've been out of the city, the South, once with him." She crushed out her cigarette. "God!—I've never been so shook before in my life. Things can't go on like this indefinitely. I'm constantly afraid someone will find out and I'll lose my job, or there'll be a scandal, or something! I'm tired of slipping around. He loves me, I'm sure of it, and I love him —but I can't go on feeling like a whore, a concubine. Slipping around, always slipping around. In public, at meetings and things, we can't let on as if we know each other intimately, I'm ignored. Oh, he lets on to me in little unrecognizable ways, but it's still illicit, makes me feel cheap and dirty—I don't feel like a woman. I want to get out of the South. But he won't leave. He has his family to worry about—his father and his damn business. I simply do not know what to do. I can't sleep at night for thinking about him. It doesn't irritate you for me to talk about him this way, does it? I mean a white man, a Southerner."

"No, I'm a Negro, but I'm beyond that kind of jealousy. My ego is free."

"Well, a lot of Negroes here would kill me if they

knew. Ha, I suppose the whites would do as much to him."

"You are a beautiful woman. Cigarette?"

"No." She did not smoke my brand. I left the table to get her a package of filter-tips. When I returned someone she knew had joined her. My interview ended. I have not been to that city since, but I have never ceased to wonder about her. Any day I expect someone to touch me from behind, on the subway, on 42nd Street, at some meeting or party, and it will be her.

Many Southerners to whom I have talked in the North have recited scores of such affairs between black women and white men in the South. The affairs are always "underground." The man and woman meet at odd hours in some deserted place, some secret rendezvous. Occasionally, the parties fall so deeply in love that they "escape" North, where they marry and raise a family. I am now thinking of Charlyne Hunter, the first black co-ed at the University of Georgia, and her southern-born classmate, who are now married.

What I am getting at is this. The white man in the South can express himself as a human being (especially sexually!) only in private. In public he must reflect the inhumanity of his culture. I suspect that much of the animosity whites heap upon blacks stems from their private disgust at their own public conduct toward blacks, especially black females. It is a terrible strain on the human personality for any man to have to act toward women according to the ethics of southern Jim Crow. Discussing his affair with the black maid who cleaned his office, one Southerner made the following "confession":

. . . In private I loved her. She was warm and exciting and I cared for her like I would for any woman. But in public I had to treat her like any other Negra. I couldn't stand it; I found myself hating her for being a colored woman. Most of all, I felt like a louse. . . .

If we assume that the white man is a human being with feelings and emotions like any other person, it inescapably follows that the "southern way of life" extracts from the southern white man a price as inhuman as that which it extracts from the African-American. Although he has some access to the black female, the white man in the South is made to feel like a sexual deviant when he experiences warmth and desire in his heart for a black woman. Because of his environment, he cannot submit freely to her, he must rape her. He cannot feel proud of the fact that he loves a black woman. He must look upon the relationship as pillage and illicity.

It stands to reason that if many Southerners could be absolved from "self-incrimination," a different story would be told than the one we hear regularly. For it is predominantly the black woman who has managed, God knows how, to maintain those qualities that all men need and yearn for. The southern white man knows this. He has known it for three centuries. Through the years, the Southerner's house, his laundry, his food, have all been attended to largely by black women. Southerners have been suckled and nursed by black breasts from infancy to boyhood. They have been warmed by black thighs from boyhood into manhood.

I recall, as a youth, visiting my grandmother at the home of her employer. There she sat, on the front porch, old and black, with one white baby in her lap, happy as an angel, and another little white boy nestling close to her thigh.

It is not easy to sever the incestuous nexus. What is even more difficult, if not impossible, is to eradicate the guilt from the conscience. I know a Southerner who is a novelist and a poet, living now in New York. Because of his background and because I respect his writing skill and experience, I went to him with a draft of one of the chapters of this book for his scrutiny and advice. Everything went well until he came to this passage:

> If the white racist has an incestuous urge for black women because of the infantile or boyhood memory of his black mammy who nursed and suckled him on her big, black breasts, I think it is reasonable to explore the possibility of some Negroes relating to white women on the same principle.

The novelist became terribly excited. He was not at all concerned with the last part of the statement, it was the first part that disturbed him. He disagreed with it vehemently, claiming that it was untrue. "White boys in the South no longer have mammies. That went out with slavery, and even then there was not much of it," he insisted. "I know, I'm a southern white. There may be maids, but no more mammies. Even during slavery it was only the rich planters who could afford mammies for their children."

The idea was too farfetched for him. He crossed out the sentence then and there on the page without waiting for my reply. But he did not stop talking about it. After nearly fifteen minutes of expounding on what the South was and is really like in its attitude toward black women, he (evidently forgetting his original stand) began telling me how honorably the maid in his father's house was treated.

"Why, she was just like one of the family," he declared, gesturing. "In fact, she ruled the house. She told my mother what to do—and, good Lord, I've seen her and my father stand up and argue for hours. And not once did I ever hear my father call her a nigger, or treat her with disrespect in any way. And, as I've told you before, my father was a bigot if ever there was one—he lynched a Negro once."

"Look," I said, "why do you think the maid was able to have free reign in your house, especially with your father?"

"Because—as they say—in the North the Negro is loved as a race and hated as a person, whereas in the South the Negro may be hated as a race but he is loved as a person."

That was a stereotyped explanation, a cliché. It seemed to have rolled out of his mouth without the control of his brain. "Listen," I looked him in the eye, "the most likely explanation—and I can cite you ten scholars who'll bear me out—is that your father was intimate with that maid. Was he, as far as you know?"

"Why, yes," he said, matter of factly. And then, as if he could not stop his tongue, added, "And when I grew up I had her too."

I did not press him further. My point was established, and I maneuvered the discussion along other lines.

If Freudians are right about the Oedipus Complex, it is an equally sound idea to hypothesize a "Dual Oedipus" when we deal with the Southerner. *One mother* *white . . . another "mother" black (the mammy or maid). . . . Where do we go from here? . . . The Southerner wishes to have relations with his white mother (Oedipus), but she is white, lily white, the epitome of all virtues and taboos. Indeed, the white mother represents all white women . . . white women symbolize sexual restraint, discipline, denial of pleasure . . . white women are lovely but not carnally lovable; they are more like the Virgin Mary. . . . But there is the maid or mammy . . . the black mother figure (Dual Oedipus), at once the real thing and a substitute. The black mother represents all black women. . . . Black women symbolize sexual freedom, promiscuity, maternal warmth, and carnal gratification. Black women are not only "loose" and touchable, they are more or less defenseless. . . . The trans-*ference is set in motion: *The black woman becomes the object in and through which the repressed Oedipus desire of childhood and the sexual frustration of manhood can be*—with little social consequence—*acted out.*

In every southern white man, whether a racist or not, there is, just below the level of awareness, the twilight urge to make love to a black woman, to sleep with the alter mother, to consume her via the act of intercourse, thereby affirming his childhood affinity for black flesh and repudiating the interracial conflict of his masculinity. Because of Jim Crow and racism, whatever genuine sexual desires the Southerner might have toward black women are twisted and distorted.

History teaches that women are always included among the spoils of conquest and domination. Everywhere, when the invading tribe or nation conquers another people, the dominating group invariably takes free liberties with females of the subjugated group. In the case of the white racists and the African-American, there is something much deeper than mere conquest and subjugation. Sexual paranoia is an inextricable ingredient in that psychiatric terror known as racism. And this fear, this guilt and terror, in various forms, is directed towards and acted out against *both* sexes of the black population.

I have never seen a lynching, never looked upon a black man who has been castrated. I understand, however, and *know*, that it is a terrible sight. The following is an account told to me by a young Negro in Mississippi:

I must have been about seven years old. No, I was about nine. . . . Anyway, I will never forget it. I can still see him hanging up like that. I was living with my uncle out on his farm. The night of the lynching, my uncle walked up and down the floor, rubbing his hands together, and he made me keep quiet everytime I woke up. He tried to make me go back to sleep, but the noise and racket they made kept me woke most of the night too. The next morning my uncle and me and some other colored folks in the county went to look at the man who had been lynched. The man's wife and brother were with us, and they were crying. Everybody was afraid. I wasn't —for I really didn't know what to expect. But maybe I was a little scared just because of all the racket that went on that night. Anyway, when we got there in the woods, everyone started crying and turning their heads away in horror. I looked up at the man. I knew him, yet he was so messed up I could not tell who he was. He was naked, and they had put tar on him and burnt him. He smelled awful. Then I saw what they had done. Even though I was only nine, I knew what they had done was a sin. They had cut out his private and left it laying on the ground. The blood was caked all about his legs and thighs. . . .

There is in the psyche of the racist (the majority of American white men are racists) an inordinate disposition for sexual atrocity. He sees in the African-American the essence of his own sexuality, that is, those qualities that he wishes for but fears he does not possess. Symbolically, the Negro at once affirms and negates the white man's sense of sexual security. The racist is torn by repressed dreams of sexual virility. On the other hand, he is secretly haunted by fantasies of masculine inadequacy, because he cannot (due to his guilt and his involvement with sex as dirty and vile) bring himself to act out his great dreams with the white woman. The racist *needs* the black to hate, blame, and fear. This is the only way he can keep from overtly hating, blaming and fearing himself. If the black did not exist the racist would be compelled to *invent* him. Indeed, this is precisely what the racist has done. It is quite clear that few, if any, of the characteristics that white men attribute to blacks are universally accurate. Contrary to what is claimed, it is not the white woman who is dear to the racist. It is not even the black woman toward whom his real sexual rage is directed. It is the black *man* who is *sacred* to the racist. And this is why he must castrate him.

The racist is so terrified of himself as an individual that he dares not think of himself or of anything as a particular entity. He thinks of himself as a generality. He is the "white race." Likewise, the Negro is not a man but a concept. He is the "black race." To be white is to be *everything* white. To be black is to be *everything* black. The white man says: "Now that I have an object like the nigger, I do not have to feel guilty or responsible for any of my sins and weaknesses. Everything that goes wrong with my life, every immoral thought and act that I commit, I can blame on the nigger—I can lynch him for my own crimes and feelings of inadequacy."

It is in this way that the racist visits his own essence upon the black—but it is not a way that leads out. For no sooner has the white man created the Negro as the guilt image—the dark, savage counterpart of himself—than he begins to envy what he has created. Sexually, in particular, he wants to *be* a Negro. He wants to enjoy the unbounded sexual vigor that he imagines blacks enjoy. White people, North and South, seem markedly interested in black sexual behavior. They exchange jokes about black sexuality with astounding vicarious pleasure. John Dollard tells of an incident where a group of white men were going through a cornfield and ". . . came upon a Negro couple having intercourse. When the men came back, they were laughing at this and one of them said, 'That is another good reason for being a nigger!' "

Most white people in America project their own inner sexual anxieties onto the Negro to such an extent that they, especially Southerners, imagine black men have large, grotesque genitals that stand in perpetual erection. One Southerner related to me how shocked he was when he came to New York and saw black homosexuals flirting up and down 42nd Street. "I'd have never believed a Negro could be a faggot," he said. The same man told me how he had wanted to kiss a beautiful black girl, but that he was repelled and attracted at the same time. He ran away with mixed emotions. Another white man claimed that he enjoyed black women far better than he did white women, because he could "let himself go" with blacks. He felt no guilt for whatever he did with black women, but with white females he seemed to "dam up" inside.

The extent to which some white women are attracted by black lesbians is immensely revealing—even the black lesbian is a "man." It is not an uncommon sight (in Greenwich Village, for instance) to see these "men" exploiting this image of themselves to the zenith.

Because the white man has created such a mammoth sex fantasy out of the Negro, the mere presence of a black man or woman in white company serves as a sex stimulant to whites. One summer afternoon I walked into a strange bar on the Lower West Side of New York. The bar was quiet and subdued. There were about a dozen patrons standing around, all white. The only female there was the barmaid, who looked rather worn and unattractive. While I was there the entire atmosphere changed—and I was not there long. One man who seemed effeminate put coins in the jukebox, swished up alongside of me, and began to shuffle his feet and snap his fingers. Some of the others started going through the motions of dancing. The whole place became vibrant. The music was by a black singer, the dance motions were imitations of what they must have taken for "Negro dancing." Everybody had their eyes trained on me, began to look towards me as I sat quietly sipping my beer. The barmaid came down to my end of the bar and began popping her fingers and wiggling her hips. A drunken man came from his place at the bar and began to hug, kiss, and fondle the barmaid—I averted my eyes from them. I imagined that that woman must have been thankful I happened along, for I am certain that no one had taken on over her like that in some time. I walked out.

To most white people, the black person *exhumes* sexuality. The racist is so full of fear, so twisted sexually, that even a young boy like Emmett Till was murdered and mutilated for speaking to a white woman in a department store.

Several years ago in South Carolina there was the infamous case of a seven-year-old child who was arrested for a playful kiss he placed on the mouth of a little white girl while they were playing together.

The white man—the Southerner—secretly worships and fears the sex image he has created in the Negro; therefore, he must destroy that image. Castration represents not only the destruction of a mythical monster, but also the *partaking* of that monster. It is a disguised form of worship, a primitive pornographic divination rite—and a kind of homosexualism in reverse. In taking the black man's genitals, the hooded men in white are amputating that portion of themselves which they secretly consider vile, filthy, and most of all, inadequate. At the same time, castration is the acting out of the white man's guilt for having sex with black women, and of the white man's hatred and envy of the black man's supposed relations with and appeal to the white woman. And finally, through the castration rite, white men hope to acquire the grotesque powers they have assigned to the black phallus, which they symbolically extol by the act of destroying it.

Why, after all, is the white man in the South so preoccupied with the black man's penis, and with black men "raping" white women! It is nothing to catch white men (and women, too, of course) in the South secretly eying the front of black men's pants. On the street, in department stores, in buses and other public places, it is incredible to suddenly realize how thoroughly and constantly aware whites are of the black man's sexual existence—an awareness, affirmed and denied, that dominates and sexualizes the entire range of race relations in the South and in the nation. If the white man is so insistent that, at the twitch of a skirt even, the black man will be after white women, then the white man must, undoubtedly, yearn deep in the shadows of his soul for the black man and the white woman to *be* intimate. There is no other explanation.

I know of a case—and there are countless others like it —where a black youth in Tennessee was picked up while playing in the park and arrested, for supposedly breaking into a beauty salon. The proprietor, a white woman, was living in the rear of the beauty parlor. They took him to police headquarters and drilled him to get a "confession." When the boy refused to "confess," they approached the white woman. The youth relates the following:

. . . I could hear them outside of the room where they kept me, trying to get the woman to cooperate with them. But she was not sure, and she would not say I was the one. They then suggested that maybe I had tried to rape her. She wouldn't go along with that either. She got mad, I think, and left the police station. Later on the cops let me go free, but before they did, they made me take off my clothes, and I had to show them my sex. One of them spilled coffee on me. He pretended it was an accident, but I don't believe him. They said if they ever caught me messing around with one of their women they would fix me for life.

The most blatant of the cultural stereotypes about blacks is the myth of Negro sexual virility. A person living in the South—the North notwithstanding—learns through jokes, anecdotes, through mores and folklore, that blacks are oversexed. Blacks exist in a savage state of "promiscuity." In 1961 the Louisiana legislature cut off thousands of Negro welfare cases on the bases of this myth. Other legislators, North and South, and social workers have proposed similar measures. There is also the notion that love-making between blacks must be a terribly vulgar sight. Therefore, blacks cannot make love on the screen; they cannot kiss or hug with passion. It would cause a riot on Broadway and a panic in Mississippi. While Paul Newman and Joanne Woodward, in *Paris Blues*, were shown lying in bed for days and nights, Sidney Poitier and Diahann Carroll must settle for a tight, but not too tight, hand squeeze. In addition to being a personality attribute of all white supremacists, the lewd concept of black sexhood is a property of American culture. Like a pervasive chemical, it is *out there* in the air, and it is difficult for any of us to keep our lungs completely free of it.

Most white men, liberals as well as racists, cannot stand the "shock" of a black man associating with a white woman. Gilbert Cross published an article in *Look* ("A White Man Looks at the Negro," Dec. 7, 1962) in which he "confessed" that when he saw a white girl "walk through the door with her Negro beau, I felt a sudden bash of anger at her for betraying a life and a

119

code we both knew . . . at him for trying to intrude upon us." Later in the same article Mr. Cross stated that his father, who spent a great deal of his energy helping blacks achieve equality, was indignant when a hotel turned away blacks, but was outraged when a black man married a white girl. Even an intellectual like Norman Podhoretz, the editor of *Commentary*, has not completely extricated himself from certain anxiety-inducing emotions when it comes to the black physical body. In an article which appeared in *Commentary* ("My Negro Problem—and Ours," February 1963) he writes: ". . . just as in childhood I envied Negroes for what seemed to be their superior masculinity, so I envy them today for what seems to be their superior grace and beauty." He goes on to say,

I am now capable of aching with all my being when I watch a Negro couple on the dance floor, or a Negro playing baseball or basketball. They are on the kind of terms with their own bodies that I should like to be on with mine, and for that precious quality they seemed blessed.

I do not know what is causing Mr. Podhoretz, a man I respect very much, to cling to such one-sided notions about the African-American. Considering white men like Bob Cousy, Gene Conley, Roger Maris, Gene Kelly, and others too numerous to cite, Podhoretz should not be alarmed because a few blacks seem to excel in sports and dancing. I am certain that if he should see me on the dance floor, he would not ache from anything but laughter.

In New York, where there is more tolerance for mixed couples than anywhere else in the United States, a black

man and a white woman cannot walk down the street
without the leering, disapproving stares of passers-by,
especially white men. The couple may know each other
only slightly or as fellow employees, it makes no difference; out of the hot eyes of those who look leaps the
sexual outrage of obscene minds. "What do you want
with that dirty nigger?" whispered a red-faced man as he
brushed past me and a white woman on the street. The
woman was my professor and we happened to be on our
way to class—and she was old enough to be my grandmother.

I cannot begin to stress the importance of obscenity in
the mind of the white man when it comes to "his"
women and the black man. Again, Podhoretz, a Jew, and
a liberal, expressed himself clearly on this point in the
above-mentioned article. He knows that his childhood
hatred for blacks has not disappeared, because, "I know
it from the disgusting prurience that can stir in me at the
sight of a mixed couple. . . ." In response to that terribly revealing question—"Would You Like Your Sister To
Marry One?"—Podhoretz makes the following confession:

> When I was a boy and my sister was still unmarried, I would
> certainly have said no to that question. Now I am a man . . .
> and I have daughters. If I were to be asked today whether I
> would like a daughter of mine to marry one, I would have to
> answer: No, I would not *like* it at all. I would rail and rave and
> tear my hair. Then I hope I would have the courage to curse
> myself for raving and ranting, and give her my blessings. . . .

So much for Podhoretz's "hopeful courage."

When it comes to sex with the black man, nearly all

121

white men in America look upon the white woman as "their" woman. When a black man is intimate with *one* white woman, in the minds and emotions of the white man, that black man is intimate with *all* white women. It is reasonable for a man to be jealous of his wife, or of a particular woman whom he knows personally. But it becomes a different matter when a man is envious and jealous of a whole race of women—women he does not know nor may never even have laid eyes on. Something is terribly wrong with such a man, he has a "sex problem" that probably no psychiatrist can solve.

Despite the stereotype of oversexed blacks bent on "polluting" the white race, which is so prevalent in the South, there is also the notion that the black man should lose his mammoth sexuality in the presence of white women; he is supposed to become sexless. While whites can be sexually aroused by all women, black and white, the black male must act as if he is not affected by white women. When I was a boy I worked with a white man on a delivery truck. I was his helper. As we rode around the city, he looked freely and made comments about the anatomy of the women we passed, especially black women, always with a vulgar note in whatever he said. I had to grin and bear this. But if an exciting white woman passed our view and I glanced at her, he would snap: "Boy, what are you looking at?" Whereupon I had to drop my head and say, "Nothing."

Ascribing to the black man a distorted sexhood and at the same time expecting him to become sexless in the presence of white women, is a reflection of the white man's own sexual ambivalence. Like any paranoiac, the racist experiences himself as an authentic individual only when he projects his fears onto others and imagines they are attacking him. In Germany the "others" were Jews. In America they are blacks. But, like the imagined attack, the racist's experience of himself as a meaningful person while he is attacking blacks is also a form of delusion. Whether the white supremacist is sexually virile or not, he *fears* he is inadequate, and he feels guilty about his fear—he therefore says blacks are oversexed. The racist *fears* his sexuality is sinful, immoral. He therefore creates, out of the black female and black male, objects of degradation upon which he can act out his own feelings of iniquity and vulgarity. The racist *fears* that the relationships between black men and women are healthier and freer than those between himself and white women. He also *fears* that black men can be better with white women than he is. He therefore transforms the white woman into a "lily lady," no longer a woman, but an idol, and he fills her with *his* paranoid fears of black men. And, finally, as he craves to maim the black man, the racist acquires a false sense of superiority and justification for his actions by imagining that the black man is bent on deflowering the symbol of his guilt and inadequacy—"sacred white womanhood."

FIVE

The Black Woman

I am quite aware of the fact that from time to time in America various individuals and groups besides blacks have been victims of prejudice, discrimination, injustice, persecution, and outright murder. I am referring to American Indians, Poles, Jews, Mexicans, Puerto Ricans, labor groups, anarchists, and so on. But it has been the black woman, more than anyone else, who has borne the constant agonies of racial barbarity in America, from the very first day she was brought in chains to this soil. The black woman through the years has suffered (and endured) every sexual outrage (with all of the psychological ramifications) that a "democratic" society can possibly

125

inflict upon a human being. The sexual atrocities that the black woman has suffered in the United States, South and North, and what these atrocities have done to her personality as a female creature, is a tale more bloody and brutal than most of us can imagine. I believe it was a black woman who first uttered the words: "Nobody knows the trouble I've seen."

As slaves black women were brought to the New World, specifically North America, for only one reason —to serve as breeding animals for more slaves. Simultaneously they served as body toys for their white masters. True, black women performed many other tasks during slavery. They worked in the fields, cooked, ironed, served as servants and nurses. But these roles were secondary. Their white masters, as Lillian Smith writes:

. . . mated with these dark women whom they had dehumanized in their minds, and fathered by them children who, according to their race philosophy, were "without souls"—a strange exotic new kind of creature whom they made slaves of and . . . sold on the auction block.[1]

It is important to understand the "race philosophy" of the ante-bellum South and how this philosophy affected the sexuality of the black woman. Black people were not considered to be human beings. They were wild, savage creatures "without souls." Negro women were *forced* to give up their bodies like animals to white men at random! Cash writes:

. . . the Negro woman . . . *torn* from her tribal *restraints* and *taught* an easy complaisance for commercial reasons, was

[1] Lillian Smith, *Killers of the Dream* (Garden City, New York: Doubleday Anchor Books, 1961), p. 103.

126

to be had for the taking. Boys on and about the plantation inevitably learned to use her, and having acquired the habit, often continued it into manhood and even after marriage. . . .[2]

Being *torn* from the sexual restraints of her native culture (Africa) and universally *forced* to behave like a "naked savage," the relatively restrained African woman was transformed sexually into a beast. Ultimately, after experiencing the ceaseless sexual immorality of the white South, the black woman became "promiscuous and loose," and could be "had for the taking." Indeed, she came to look upon herself as the South viewed and treated her, for she had no other morality by which to shape her womanhood, she had no womanhood so far as the white South was concerned. And make no mistake, it was the whole of the South who so used her and not merely "southern white trash."

Repeatedly, people who visited the ante-bellum South were shocked to find such striking resemblances between the white master of the house and some of his black slaves. Those black women (and there were many) who tried to maintain a measure of dignity in regard to their sex were beaten, burned, lynched, and treated worse than dogs. For example, no law was violated when, in 1838, a North Carolina slaveowner admitted that he burnt the left side of a black woman's face with a hot iron, which caused her to run away with her two boys, one of whom was as light as the slaveowner. The same slaveowner admitted branding the letter "R" on the

[2] W. J. Cash, *The Mind of the South* (New York: Vintage Books, 1960), p. 87. My italics.

127

cheek of a sixteen-year-old black girl; he also cropped a piece of her ear, and branded the same letter on the *inside* of both of her legs![3]

When any group of women has to submit to such atrocities, when they are denied the smallest privacy of body, when they have to stand in public before men and women naked on an auction block and be fingered in the most intimate places, it is absurd to ask them to esteem themselves as restrained ladies and conduct their sexual activities along the lines of female refinery. The fiber of the human personality is not that independent of the milieu in which it has to struggle for sanity. It was in this way, then, that the Negro woman during slavery began to develop a depreciatory concept of herself not only as a female but as a human being as well. She did not have much of an alternative.

Then came the Civil War, followed by several turbulent but most courageous years in American history—Reconstruction. Great efforts were made to lift the African-American out of his state of degradation. In modern parlance, there was an all-out drive to change the "image" of black people. Noxious laws were removed from the statute books; there were strong sanctions against polygamy and promiscuity; and for the first time marriages of black women were universally legalized. Black men began to demand that all women of color be treated with respect and courtesy, to insist that white men stop seducing and raping black women. In 1874 a black congressman proclaimed the following: "We want more

[3] See Maude White Katz, "The Negro Woman and the Law" *Freedomways*, Vol. II, No. 3, p. 282.

protection from the whites invading our homes and destroying the virtue of our women than they from us."[4]

But, alas, it was all in vain. No sooner were these measures underway, than Reconstruction ended. With the election of Hayes as President in 1876, the North compromised with the South, Union troops were withdrawn, and the black woman found herself again in the merciless hands of an embittered and barbarous South. The Ku Klux Klan, the Knights of the White Camellia, and other such hate groups spread like wildfire throughout the South. Rapes of black women were as common as "whistling 'Dixie.' "

From 1891 to 1921 the South lynched forty-five Negro women, several of whom were young girls from fourteen to sixteen years old. (This was the number of lynchings acknowledged!) . . . One victim was in her eighth month of pregnancy. Members of the mob suspended her from a tree by her ankles. Gasoline was poured on her clothes and ignited. A chivalrous white man took his knife and split open her abdomen. The unborn child fell to the ground. A member of the mob crushed its head with his heel. . . . Another victim was burned at the stake with her husband before a crowd of one thousand persons. . . .[5]

No, these things did not happen in Nazi Germany, thirteenth-century Europe, or during the time that Voltaire wrote *Candide*. They took place in the South, in the United States of America, in the nineteenth and twentieth centuries! Add to this the fact that, after the failure and betrayal of Reconstruction by the North,

[4] Ibid., p. 283.
[5] Ibid., p. 284.

129

thousands of black men were left helpless and hopeless, uneducated and without any means of securing a livelihood. Their property was taken, and their citizenship was denied. The South succeeded in taking out its grief and bitterness against the African-American in every way possible.

Consequently the black woman in the South was left without any protection whatever. Even if a black man were around when a white man seduced, insulted, or raped his woman, what could he do, unarmed and outnumbered as he was? So once more the black woman was beaten back into slavery. Once more she became a sex toy and a domestic peon. She scrubbed floors, washed and ironed dirty clothes, cooked and served the white South's food. She suckled and reared the white South's children, and she was "had" almost for the taking by any white man who desired her. She must have been a strong creature with the resignation of a saint, for, while she did these things for the white South, she also maintained her own shack and supported and fought with her "shiftless" black man. She brought up her own children—the sons to be, if not lynched, "castrated" in one way or another by the ethic of living Jim Crow; the daughters to be the body toys of white men. And, somehow, she survived—she sang the gospel all day Sunday and moaned the blues throughout the week. From Bessie Smith, Mammy Yancey and Mamie Smith, right on down to Billie Holiday and Mahalia Jackson, there is no one in the world who can bring tears to your eyes like a black woman singing the blues.

It is against this historical, socioeconomic, and moral backdrop that the sexual behavior of the black woman

130

must be analyzed. When one considers the fact that (until recently) the major area of employment open to Negro women has been in the field of domestic service, it is easy to understand why and how so many black women have engaged in sexual relations with white men. Such relations may be viewed as a sort of "occupational hazard." Even today, throughout the entire South, white men are able to extort sexual pleasures from black women in the course of the women's employment, or in the course of their seeking employment.

The same trend may be observed in the North. There are numerous "employment agencies" that specialize in "recruiting" black girls from the South by glamorous advertising (i.e., the agencies offer to pay the train fare, promise high salaries in rich white Northern homes, etc.). There are several such agencies in Manhattan and the surrounding suburbs. Many of the young girls who respond to these alluring offers are soon disillusioned and end up in one of the northern ghettos such as Harlem or Southside Chicago. They turn into prostitutes, welfare cases, or outright derelicts. One tall, dark, tough-faced girl of about twenty-two, stated:

. . . damn white folks up here act just like the crackers down South. They want you to cook, wash, be a mammy, and fuck 'em too. The hell wit it—I'll carry my black butt back to Georgia first. At least down there I know where I stand.

On the other hand, the black woman may "take advantage" of the situation. Like any other woman, the black woman may "play along" with white men to obtain money, employment, and other "gains." But especially in the South (the North notwithstanding), much more is usually involved than mere "playing along." The white man, according to the overt mores of the South, is taboo as a husband for a black woman. A tension is therefore set up in the black woman when she is in his presence. She experiences temptation for the forbidden. Moreover, there is a more human element that tends to draw the black woman towards the white man. She works with and handles objects that are his personal possessions. She nurses his children, cooks his food, darns his socks, washes his underwear, and spends long hours in his home. In a laundry or a restaurant, too, the black woman works *around* white men, or she works with things that belong to the white man's *person*. A kind of symbolic or vicarious intimacy ensues which may create an unconscious desire in the black woman to actually experience the white man—and, despite her seemingly negative attitude, she may be waiting and hoping for his advance. Sexual contact with the white man may represent a way of "getting back" at his wife, or at white women in general. Dollard reports that a black woman informed him that one of her friends "slept in the very bed of the white man's wife without the wife's knowledge." He further stated that there may be the feeling of pulling the white man down, making him "come off his high perch," and showing him to be, after all, just another human being.[6]

More than once I have overheard black women in the South boasting among themselves about how well such and such a white man treats them, or about how they have secretly "wedded" such and such a white man to

[6] John Dollard, *Caste and Class in a Southern Town* (Garden City, New York: Doubleday Anchor Books, 1949), p. 153.

132

their apron strings, more securely than the man's own wife. And they laugh about it mockingly. For the black woman is aware that the white man believes that all black women are great sexual animals who cannot only satisfy him better than any white woman but also who can release him from whatever complexes that may be repressing his sexuality. The white Southerner may treat black women with the utmost contempt in public, but the black woman knows the difference between the public white man and the private white man. Then, too, there is not a "good-looking" black woman in the South who has not been sexually approached by a white man.

In a large cosmopolitan southern city there is a very voluptuous but unattractive black woman. She drives a new Cadillac every year, owns a beautiful house, and wears the most expensive clothes in the city. This woman has no visible means of support. The blacks whisper about her, laugh, and make jokes. "That black fat mamma got her mo-jo working on a white man downtown," they all say—some with contempt, some with laughter, and the women usually with envy. Without a doubt, this phenomenon is repeated throughout the South.

The personality, or *ego*, of the black woman is a product of and a *response* to all of the historical forces of American society. Among these forces, racism, or white supremacy, has had the most powerful effect, shaping both the way whites treat and conceive of the black woman, and the very attitudes that black women have towards themselves.

Recently a young black girl published an article in which she stated:

[America] You are my country. I am yours. You have made me, have created me out of yourself, but you do not want me. You have belittled and degraded me until I have become little and degraded. You have not believed in me, until I no longer believe in myself. You have not accepted me, until I no longer accept myself.[7]

A tragic majority of black women in America, in the most fragile corners of their egos, feel degraded, belittled, and are haunted by a nagging sense of self-rejection —simply because they are colored and have Negroid features and have been led to believe a propaganda of history in which they can find no glory or dignity for themselves as females. Because the black woman has been and is judged, by whites and blacks alike, according to the Caucasian standard of beauty and femininity, the African-American woman hates herself. What does the Negro woman feel when she looks into the mirror, the actual mirror as well as the mirrors of other people's faces? How does her sensory perception play her image back to her ego? Being dark and Negroid, she sees a *negative;* she feels a mixture of racial-sexual-feminine emotions that fractures her personality to splinters. And she knows that her man feels the same way, or worse, about her. At the same time, she demands from her black man the utmost in terms of the very standards that have created in her this despicable concept of herself. She asks the black man for absolute loyalty, great practical

[7] Jane Rogers Clay, "Goodbye America," *Negro Digest*, October 1963, p. 11.

134

achievement, ultimate security (a good job and money), nice fragile decency—in general, she wants her man to treat her as she thinks white men treat their wives. The black man, in his turn, responds with an attitude which says (or he actually says): "Woman you must think you're white! But if you were white you wouldn't be so mean all the time and you'd understand my problems in this world, and would be loving and kind just like white women are towards their men!" So what we have is an impasse.

Black men and women "fuss and fight" constantly, because the values of the white supremacist's world invade their lives from sunup to sundown, even into the coupling of their loins at night. Nothing is free from the effects of the sexualization of racism. They call each other "nigger" more frequently and with more contempt than many Southerners would do. For when they look at one another, they see and feel what they have been taught to see and feel about blacks—something that is esthetically repulsive.

> Looking in her looking-glass
> At the unembroidered brown
> Printing bastard roses there;
> Then emotionally aware
> Of the black and boisterous hair,
> Taming all that anger down.[8]

Thumb through any magazine or publication that caters to the "African-American market," and you will be

[8] Gwendolyn Brooks, *Selected Poems* (New York: Harper & Row, 1963), p. 39. It will interest the reader to know, if he does not already, that Miss Brooks is a black woman, and the only black poet to be awarded the Pulitzer Prize.

amazed at the nature of the ads. In *Ebony* magazine, for instance, there are ads ranging from skin "lighteners" to hair "straighteners." One ad in particular pictures a black woman with long, black "Caucasian hair" that falls down over her frail "Caucasian shoulders"—the ad is for a product called "Silky Straight." Although the model in the ad is dark-complexioned, her skin is smooth as silk and her features are as keen and fragile as blades of grass. One black woman, Madame Walker, has amassed a fortune by selling products to blacks that are supposed to make them look Caucasian. Even the fashion models in black publications are seemingly chosen on the basis of how close they approximate the frail, slim, small-breasted Caucasian archetypes found in such magazines as *Harper's Bazaar, Seventeen,* and so on. It seems that the "organization men" of the ad world are molding the psychology of black women in regard to beauty and sex appeal to an alien image—the image of the petite, piously pornographic white woman. Recently a black woman has been seen in a television commercial for a New York bank. The woman is Diahann Carroll, and the lights shine upon her so brightly that if I did not know Miss Carroll was black I would think she was a white woman.

The attempt to become "white" intensifies rather than mitigates the black woman's frustration in a white world. No amount of paint, powder, and hair straightener can erase all the things in the black woman's background that make her black, let alone transform her facial and body features into Caucasian features. Such feature-transforming potions merely distort the black woman's biological features. More important, they distort and intensify the black woman's concept of her femininity and esthetic appreciation of herself as a beauty capable of attracting men. The black woman becomes ashamed of what she is and hates what she is not. For she knows—how can she but help know!—that there are *real* white women out there in the world, and that their reality, their *whiteness* has been mythologized into something called "sacred white womanhood"—a myth of virtue, purity, beauty, and, recently, sex appeal. All of this negates these qualities in the black woman and plagues and terrifies her sexual esteem incessantly.

White society's denial of the qualities of beauty, sex appeal, and intelligence in black women is illustrated in an incident related by Constance Baker Motley, a brilliant legal counselor who formerly worked for the NAACP. Mrs. Motley, a compellingly handsome woman, unmistakably black, was arguing a case in a Mississippi courtroom. A white man walked over to her and said: "I know you ain't no nigger; you must be Indian."

Here are some lines written by Jane Rogers Clay, a young black girl.

I . . . knew that I was wrong to be black and I was sorry that I was black. I knew that black children were not as good as white children, or as smart, or as pretty . . .[9]

Such simple candor, such innocent insight. Relating what happened and how she felt when she entered an all-white school, Jane Clay continues:

When I sit down no one sits beside me. One day a girl moved when I sat down. The next day she put her purse and

[9] Clay, op. cit., p. 12.

her scarf and her books on the chairs around her. . . . When I am with them I feel very very black, very very stupid, very very inferior. When they laugh, I think they are laughing at me. . . . I do not like to feel this way. I want to cry, to scream, to hit them, all of them who make me feel this way. But I cannot cry, that would show weakness. I cannot scream, that would show madness. I cannot hit them, that would show rashness. *So I hate them for making me feel this way. And I hate myself for feeling this way. And I hate my country. I hate America for making me hate.*[10]

Not every black woman is as honest as Jane Clay. But whether they admit it or not, at some point in every black woman's life she experiences a maddening hatred for the white woman, her alter image of self-negation. And, since one cannot scream, cannot hit, cannot destroy or actually become the alter image and all that it stands for, the hatred is turned upon oneself, and it affects whatever relations exist between black women and black men. For, as the black woman hates herself, she is aware that the black man loathes her also, and for the same reason—being black. Black women and men learn, throughout their lives, to cope with and live with this smoldering self-resentment. But the toll it takes of their sense of sexual worth (not to mention the other aspects) is immeasurable. For instance, many black women simply cannot be comfortable in the presence of white females. They grow tense and nervous, and anxiety stirs in them. They experience an undefined threat to their egos as sexual creatures.

[10] Ibid., p. 14. My italics.

One of the most charming, sensitive, intelligent Negro women I know, tells me that even now when she is . . . with white people she grows physically ill and has immense difficulty coming to terms with the resentment of her childhood.[11]

I suspect that the deeper meaning in the practice of many black women in the South of beating their children (especially the boys) to a point of sheer exhaustion is to be found somewhere in the pent-up rage that black women have in their hearts against white women and against a sociosexual morality that denies black women the right to be beautiful, loving, and idealized by black and white men alike.

The cumulative effects of the way black women have been mistreated and sexually dehumanized in America, the way they have had to labor to earn a living and rear children and support both white and black men, from the days of slavery even until now, have produced in many black females a sort of "stud-ism," which expresses itself in a strong matriarchical drive. Black men complain that black women are too dominating, too demanding, too strict, too inconsiderate, and too "masculine"—so much so that the men get the feeling that they are being "castrated." Well, what can one expect? After all, throughout the entire span of her existence on American soil, the black woman has been alone and unprotected, not only socially but psychologically as well. She has *had* to fend for herself as if she were a man; being black, even more so. I am not implying that the black woman has become frigid or "masculine." In fact, she is potentially, if not already, the most sexual animal on this

[11] Smith, op. cit., p. 130.

planet. It is not frigidity that I am describing. It is *rigidity*. And it has been this quality of austerity in the black woman which has enabled her to survive what few other women have ever lived through, and which has produced, against mammoth odds, such black women as Harriet Tubman, Sojourner Truth, Mary McCloud Bethune, Bessie Smith, Margaret Walker, Georgia Douglas, Marian Anderson, Gloria Richardson, Shirley Graham, and, to mention one more, a little dark girl with pigtails who braved a mob of screaming maniacs in Little Rock, Arkansas.

I have in my possession a mimeographed paper of approximately 3700 words; the title of the paper is, "White Woman, Black Man, Black Woman." Recently copies of this paper were distributed on the Lower East Side of New York, where, of late, a cultural revival has been launched among the young black and white intellectuals who live in the area. Recipients of the paper were invited to attend a forum where the issues raised in the paper would be discussed. The author is a black woman, and she begins with the following statement:

An undercurrent of agitation within the Negro community is the alarm manifested by many young Negro women at their suspected abandonment in social intercourse by growing numbers of Negro men in favor of social intercourse with and often marriage to white women.

Straight through to the end the paper decries and laments the "abandonment" of black women by black men in favor of white women. Its author bitterly opposes and denounces black men and white women for associating together; she prosecutes all black man-white woman relationships on the grounds that they are formed out of unhealthy or neurotic motivations. She contends that black men who become intimate with white women are really trying to escape from reality; they are social weaklings or sulking babies; most of all, she claims, such men are "betraying" the race as a whole and betraying the black woman in particular.

Negro women who have acquired higher educations and professional status have a problem of . . . finding mates. It is their consistent complaint that Negro men with college educations and professional status too frequently search among white women for wives. Since white men do not marry Negro women, and poorly educated Negro men are neither acceptable nor accepting, Negro women of superior achievement have their peculiar frustration to contend with.

While the paper shows some valid insights and raises some legitimate complaints, it does not reflect much analytical objectivity; nor does it get beyond the author's own race-sex frustration over interracial intimacy between black men and white women. She states, for instance, that black men who marry white women are "narcotizing themselves behind their white wives as others withdraw from responsibility behind alcohol or drugs." If such men are as "derelict" as she claims, it would seem to me that black women would do well to get them off their hands. She states, "since white men do not marry black women . . . ," which is obviously nothing more than a personal prejudice, for white men *do* marry black women! Also, throughout the paper, the author writes as if thousands of black men were "compromising the black man's integrity for the white man's

141

values" by marrying white women; then, on the final page, she writes: "While it is by no means a common problem, the number of occasions being really very few, it is a matter of tremendous irritation to those who are concerned with it who feel unjustly rejected."

And this is more like it—those who *feel* "rejected"! In the final paragraph of the paper, she writes: "The question remains of the extent to which black women are themselves responsible for their grievances. . . ." But, for some reason or other, she does not go into this question at all.

The cold statistical facts are that black women are not being abandoned by black men who marry white women any more than white women are being abandoned by white men who marry black women. Consult the records of marriage licenses over the past fifty years. Any person of either race who asserts that the reason he or she has not found a suitable lover is because the opposite sex of his or her race has "abandoned" him or her for the other race, is revealing more about his or her self than about anyone or anything else. Specifically, black women who become alarmed when they see a black man with a white woman are reacting out of the same race-sex-jealousy emotional syndrome as is a white man who is alarmed over white women and black men. At the core of their irritation is the suppressed feeling that the mixed couple is experiencing a more thrilling, if not more fruitful, sexual relationship than the onlooker is enjoying with his or her lover. Granted, the black female may "feel unjustly rejected" when a black man or several black men ignore her in favor of a white woman. What is important is the *reason* for that feeling—and the reason, when all else has been thrashed out, is usually *personal* and *sexual*. Anyway, what is "unjust rejection" in a man-woman relationship? We always feel "unjustly rejected" when we want someone and that person turns us down. I am aware, as I have indicated throughout this book, that there are forces in America that tend to make some black men pursue white women to the exclusion of black women. It seems to me, however, that black women who feel a threat to their sexuality and to the "dignity of their race" because a few blacks are marrying white women, are themselves handicapped as females in the first place.

There are terrible economic, racist, and sexual forces in the United States that have given the black woman a depraved concept of herself and have made her a "difficult" person to deal with. And contrary to what "nationalistic" blacks assert, there are black women—just as there are white women—in America who are physically and psychologically almost impossible to bear in an intimate heterosexual relationship. If I were asked for counsel, I would advise black women—indeed, everyone in America—to work for the obliteration of those forces in our society and culture that not only frustrate black men and women, but set the sexes at odds with each other in general. As Pearl Buck has lamented, nowhere in the world are men and women so estranged as in the United States.

The black woman does have a problem with her man when it comes to the white woman, but, like the black man, she also has a problem with herself when it comes to the entire American culture. There are black men who feel that they have been "unjustly rejected" when a black woman becomes intimate with a white man. As

143

long as racism, segregation, and the pseudo values of white supremacy continue, Americans will go on feeling sexual anxiety and racial rage at the sight and thought of mixed intimacy. The "race problem" becomes a vehicle, a scapegoat rationalization, a bandwagon, for what ought to be, and is, a more private concern.

The psychosexual reactions of oppressed people are one of the most intriguing and depressing things to observe. Many black women (and men) are ardent advocates of a thoroughly integrated American society; but when it comes to sex, they oppose it with as much vigor as they do the southern racist—and perhaps for the same fundamental fears. They do not know what to expect. Just as some black school principals and college presidents oppose integration in education because they think they have a vested interest in segregated institutions and that they have something *personal* to lose, so a few black women feel they have something personal to lose if sex becomes integrated. In a phrase, they have a psycho-socio-sexual vested interest in a closed world. The fact is, these women have nothing to lose in an integrated world except what they have to lose and are losing in a segregated world.

Black women who hold up the banner of "race pride" or of "unjust rejection" when they see *a* black man or *some* black men marrying white women are, in essence, not really angry about that at all—usually their anxiety and bitterness stem from the fact that they are rarely successful with men of either race under any conditions. Such women hate not just black men who associate with white women, they hate all black men—they hate all men. Such women hate not just white women who associate with black men, they hate all white women—they hate all women. Consequently, the segregated world provides them with a measure of security from open competition. Some black man, in desperation, will have to settle for them eventually, so they think. But the security is false, for it is clear that such women lead sexually disgruntled lives anyway. Their fear of competing with white women is generated by their inability to compete successfully with the women of their own race. Predominantly, the women who become most alarmed over interracial marriages are single or are victims of unhappy marriages themselves.

One informant, for instance, complained bitterly about black men who "ignored their own women to run after white trash." She said that most black men who achieved some kind of status or fame desert their own women and marry white women. She mentioned Sammy Davis, Jr., and Richard Wright, both of whom she described with the utmost hatred and contempt. When I pointed out that some black women of status and fame— Lena Horne, Pearl Bailey, Lorraine Hansberry—married white men, she said she was unaware of this, and merely shrugged her shoulders. She seemed to be totally unaware that intermarriage took place in two directions. The young lady, who was a Chicago schoolteacher, later stated that she would not become intimate with a white man, no matter how much he loved her and no matter what he could offer her. As I spoke with her in repeated interviews, I discovered that she was thirty years old, had never been married, had had several "boy friends," none of whom had ever proposed. She was shy, physically attractive, although she dressed in such a way that no one would ever notice it, rural, "formally" educated, but beyond that terribly ignorant. She considered sexual intercourse something "dirty that we women have to put up with." She was race-conscious to the point of nausea. She attended all her classes on time and was quiet and dignified whenever in the presence of whites, so that she would not "let the race down." She was always on the lookout for black men with white women, and it always made her feel "strange and disgusted." Wherever she went, her mother always came to visit her to, in the words of the informant, "see after me." She constantly reprimanded me for not exemplifying her behavior.

It is easy to see what bothers us most, but we do not often see *why* it bothers us! It seems to me that many black women who complain about black men ignoring them for white women are actually unaware that they are jealous of the attention that black men arouse in white women. The white stereotype of the black man's sex image is often the main force that draws some white females toward them. Distorted as it is, the black woman envies this image; she cannot compete with it, in reference to either white or black men, and like the white man, her ego cannot bear seeing white women and black men together. One black girl related how she tried to correct the situation. She informed her white girl friends that black men were no different from white ones, and that they should not submit to them so easily. When asked if her advice proved fruitful, she replied: "No, white women are so stupid. Sometimes I think they're all sluts or something."

The threat to the ego that all but a few black women feel in the presence of Caucasian women may be illuminated when one considers that some black females experience this same anxiety in the company of other black women. There is within the black group itself sexual jealousy and discrimination on the basis of color variations. When a dark-skinned black woman is with her husband or lover, and a light-skinned colored woman joins the company, the dark-skinned one perks up, her metabolic rate does "crazy" things to her emotions; she is on guard to make sure nothing happens between her man and the "more attractive woman." Every black woman is aware that "if you are white you are all right; if you are brown you can stick around; but if you are black . . . get back!"

A situation that ought to be of grave concern to the Black Muslims and other such groups is what to do about brown- and light-skinned blacks when the "black millennium" comes. Are they, then as now, going to advocate a sort of "black chauvinism"? Will the black African-Americans be trying to marry all of the light-skinned ones? Will the brown- and light-skinned ones organize and overthrow the black ones? It is a difficult thing to be black in America. But in sexual life, not to mention other areas, the dark-skinned woman experiences additional abuse. A dark-skinned woman is discriminated against by blacks as well as whites. "A yellow woman may be low-down, but a black one is evil," goes the saying among blacks. She is not born evil, but her chances of being genteel, loving, and personable are virtually impossible in a world that sees nothing but her color. This is why many black women in the North have developed what I call "black woman chauvinism." They have a genuine hatred for white women and the black

147

men who pursue them; they hate the sight of a light-skinned black woman. After all, black women are females, and they have the desires that all females have—for attention, for sexual gratification, for respect and reverence, for sexual self-esteem. And if they do not realize such desires, like any other woman, they tend to become "difficult personalities," "evil."

More and more of these women—the black, "ugly" ones—are beginning to revolt against racist values and against American culture. They do not want to have anything to do with a society (and its men) that relegates them to a category of "unlovables," on the basis of their being at the extreme Negroid end of the Caucasian-Negro continuum. Rather than being ashamed of their blackness, their woolly hair and heavy Negroid features, they are becoming proud of them. Attempting to overturn the white standards of beauty and femininity, they are finding standards for their beauty and lovableness in the newly emerging African nations. Proudly they wear their unstraightened hair and thick facial features free of powder and paint; and they are as certain of their beauty and attractiveness as any other woman in America, even more so, with no signs of the old inferiority feelings. They mock black men who prefer white or light-skinned women. They are attempting, with some success, to *Africanize* the standards of feminine appeal in America. And they are certain to associate with and marry only blacks who have an authentic adherence to their standards.

A distinction must be made between the truly Africanized black woman and the pseudo-Africanized black woman. There are hypocrites in all phases of American life, and the area of sex and race is no exception but the rule. Like the pseudo-Muslim male, there are black women who parade around in African regalia, with their heads uncombed, and who spout a strong "black-pride" rhetoric. But the first white opportunity that comes their way, they grab it. And here I am not referring to the native African women, the students, visitors, and diplomatic aides, who are in this country; most of these women make no bones about African nationalism and associating with white men.

The pseudo-Africanized black woman is an American Negro, native to American soil and culture. Most of them are disappointed women as far as men are concerned. They have come to believe thoroughly in the white standard of femininity; they are full of self-bitterness over being black and unwanted. They "hate" American culture because it has "unjustly rejected" them. Because they hate Negroes so deeply it is impossible for a black man to get along with them. Such women use the "exotic" dress of Africa and the *au naturel* personal appearance, plus the radical jargon of "I'm black and beautiful," as a flamboyant front to draw attention from men, especially white men. Repeatedly I have witnessed such women, after a time, catching their secret prize—a Caucasian male.

There is also the black woman who, without any pretense at Africanization, but as a matter of "personal principle," asserts vehemently that she could never become intimate with a white man. I have seen these women fall in love with white men so frequently that now when I hear one proclaim her unavailability to Caucasian males,

I am automatically tempted to inquire when she expects to marry one.

Contrary to what one might expect, among black women the orthodox middle-class woman is most violently opposed to intermarriage. By "middle-class" I mean women, married and single, whose earnings and/ or whose husbands' earnings place them above the, say, twenty-thousand-dollar income bracket. By "orthodox" I imply something about their concept of how they, and all blacks should live their lives; I imply something about their sexual outlook towards a rapidly integrating world and towards themselves as blacks who have "succeeded" in a more or less segregated world. Predominantly, orthodox middle-class black women are married to black men who have "risen" in segregated society in the traditional Negro professions—as schoolteachers, college professors, doctors, ministers, middle-echelon civil servants, lawyers, and businessmen. A majority of these women are middle-aged or older. Their position in the socioeconomic structure may be genetically referred to as the "old" black bourgeoisie, as opposed to that of the "new" middle-class blacks who are making their money from occupations and professions in an integrated atmosphere and who have a different (even *avant garde*) set of values towards the world and towards themselves as African-Americans.

What is important in isolating the orthodox middle-class black woman from the rest is not the objective economic basis for her class position, not her eighty-thousand-dollar home in "black suburbia," not her bank account, not any of her property; rather, it is her particular outlook, her *sociosexual morality* towards the race problem. By and large, one finds that these women have thoroughly internalized and accepted the values and the morality of the white, Protestant world. They have the same ideas about dress, social etiquette, charity work, political matters, private manners, and public morals as do their alter egos, from whom they have copied their style of living—white women. They share the same contempt and stereotyped views about "lower-class" blacks as the outer society. And when it comes to sex, the orthodox middle-class black woman is far more rigid, repressed, and neurotic than any other female in America.

Although she pretends to be free of race-consciousness, she is obsessed with the "uplifting" of her race, particularly in terms of "culture," of manners, morals, public behavior (especially around whites), and the "niceties" of social etiquette. She is ashamed of uneducated, boisterous, dirty Negroes—she loathes them and refers to them always as "common." The most uncomfortable thing to her is that whites put her in the same racial category as all Negroes, regardless of "cultural refinement," and especially regardless of variations in pigmentation. For the orthodox middle-class black woman is usually a "light-skinned" woman, and, indeed, it is her complexion upon which she secretly prides herself. It is her "light skin" that has enabled her to marry a professional black man (usually dark) who has lifted her to the status of "middle class."

She moves within a closed circle of black professionals and their wives, all of whom gossip about each other, sponsor social functions, attend church dutifully, send their children to the best Negro schools, and, in general, mimic the classical stereotyped mannerisms and activi-

151

ties of middle-class white women. Although she lends her support to civil rights, better job opportunities, equal education, and so on, when it comes to integration on the sexual level, she bitterly opposes it. She may verbalize her opposition in various ways—she may deny outright that whites attract blacks sexually, she may oppose it on the basis of "racial pride," or she may say that interracial marriage will "set back the struggle for African-American freedom."

Middle-class black women are terribly defensive. They abhor anything that, according to their standards (which are the standards of the white world), "reflects negatively upon the race." To most of them, becoming intimate with a white man, especially in the South where the law prohibits it, constitutes an illicity of the highest order. If there is one thing the orthodox middle-class black woman wants to uphold, it is the law (they are usually opposed to acts of civil disobedience by those in civil rights movements). Being ashamed of her race, she desires to live as inconspicuously as possible and as close as possible to what she thinks the majority of white people consider "proper" for Negroes.

Behind the middle-class black woman's opposition to interracial intimacy—behind her rationalizations and excuses—there is a deep sexual fear, even jealousy. She is usually old, or conceives of herself as such, and she is already trapped in a marriage that means nothing to her but status within the black community, on the one hand, and security from the white world, on the other. She has missed her chances of ever having a white man, no matter what changes occur in American race relations. She therefore opposes sexual integration simply because, if

152

she cannot participate in it, she does not want anyone else to do so either. Her light skin has given her the highest status a woman can reach within the segregated world, and also an advantage over other black women with black men. She thinks, correctly, that open integration would destroy these advantages, which are based after all on the very thing that integration is intended to obliterate—color prejudice. So, while middle-class black women show a driving preference for light-skinned children, they oppose sexual integration because they fear that black men of higher means will no longer have to settle for "light-skinned" black women; and they know that they themselves will have to stop "playing white" within the black community and prove themselves as desirable females.

For some time now, many of the better Negro colleges in the South have engaged in a student exchange program with several predominantly white colleges in various parts of the country. Yearly, white students come South to study for a semester in Negro institutions, and an equal number of black students go to the white institutions. It is noticeable that the white coeds have no trouble being wooed by the black men in either environment, but the black coeds, both on their own campus and on the white campus, find that the white boys do not take to them as rapidly or as aggressively as the black boys take to white girls. The emotions of jealousy (of black men), envy and hatred (of white girls) are always discernible in the castigations that black women hurl at Negro men and Caucasian females. In a culture where the women are supposed to play shy while the men are aggressive and demanding, it seems that white men are less aggressive than black men. The black woman is aware of this, and since she cannot herself become the aggressor, she has to wait patiently for the reluctant white male. Often she is not approached at all, while the white girl, thanks to the black man's sexual aggressiveness, has long since caught her black beau. Assessing this situation on every level of her consciousness, the black woman feels sexually insecure about "social" integration, and until she has got a white man already in her clutches, she screams "No" to sexual intimacy across the color line. She says she is not attracted to the white man at all; that is, until she gets one.

A kind of "proof" that black women are concerned about white men may be obtained from the fact many black women grow irritated in the mere presence of a white man; they become disturbed when they see an interracial couple, especially a black man and a white woman. Sitting with me in a New York restaurant, a young woman became nervous and jittery upon seeing a black woman and her white escort enter the restaurant. The young woman leered hostilely at the couple as they ate and chatted. Finally, unable to contain her emotions any longer, she pointed to the couple and exclaimed that she could not see how any respectable African-American could betray her race by associating with a white man. The sight was "disgusting," she said. One year later, the same young woman enrolled in a northern university and began to "betray her race" with such enthusiasm that her father came and took her away.

The dreams of many black women—especially middle-class women—reveal a suppressed sexual desire for white men. Recurrent in the dreams are such items as eating with a white man, being accidentally kissed by a white man, or actually having intercourse with one. Yet not only do these women deny their desire for white men, they have each traditionally asserted that no white man is capable of arousing sexual desire in them,

. . . until a certain man came along. When she saw him, she had the experience for the first time of being strongly drawn to a white man; she did not know why it was, but she had many daydreams and thoughts about him. Nothing was said . . . but . . . she became very rebellious against the white people who, she felt, prevented their getting together.[12]

Because of segregationist ideology in the South, which prohibits or prevents legitimate intimacy between the races, I submit that every black woman at one time or another has experienced, in some dark crevice of her being, the illicit desire for a white man; especially those women who claim the contrary. Moreover, because the personal embodiment of pride and power in America is the white man, and because the black woman has been and is denied approved sexual access to this embodiment of sociomasculine prestige, the white man's presence in her midst constitutes a nagging threat to her ego as a human female. To assert that she is not susceptible to his touch means nothing more than that the black woman is going along with what she thinks most Americans (black and white) want her to claim. In the South, due to the severe legal and nonlegal penalties dealt out to blacks who break the sex-race taboo, even in thought or desire, one is not able to see clearly, except in rare cases, what

[12] Smith, op. cit., p. 148.

the white man really means to the black woman. Blacks in the South must hide and lie about their true feelings, until it is impossible to know exactly how the black female sexually perceives the Caucasian male.

It is to the North, then, that one must turn.

Hilda is an extremely dark, tall, and very attractive young black woman about twenty-five years old. She and Fred had been married for five years at the time I formally interviewed them during the summer of 1963.[13] They have no children and are now living abroad in the country where Fred was stationed during his tour of duty in the Army. They are both native New Yorkers.

Fred and Hilda were my friends. I had known them long before I formally interviewed them for this book. I had had meals with them, gone with them to movies, parties, and other occasions where behavior was relaxed and where the ease of social intercourse provided a sort of "participant observer" setting for me. I had even spent nights in their apartment, so that I knew many subtle as well as obvious things about them. Not once, during the whole time I knew them, did I have any intention of spying on them. The true student of human nature is an habitual observer of human beings; the sociologist is obsessed with his subject matter, his faculties are instinctively tuned in on all of the nuances of human behavior, including his own, whether the setting for the behavior is an intoxicated brawl or the most austere discourse between individuals. Deep inside of every man possessed by a desire to understand why people act the

13 "Hilda" and "Fred" are real people. I have used fictitious names to make sure that their identity remains anonymous.

way they act, there is an owl who never sleeps. When I told Fred and Hilda about my plans for this book, they consented to serve as informants and gladly gave me leave to use anything I had observed about them which, at my discretion, would enhance the value of this book. The day I formally interviewed Hilda, she was to board a ship that evening which would take her thousands of miles away from her native land.

I apologized for being late.

"I almost didn't make it, myself," she said. "But I promised you, so here I am. I have about two hours." She was excited. Her beautiful black face gleamed with expectancy. The black strands of her hair swept upward in an exotic coiffure. I could not keep my eyes off her tall, shapely figure as she preceded me to a seat. As we sat at the table—she across from me—I stared into her large, shining, brown eyes; my hand instinctively reached out to touch her cheek; her well-sculptured mouth warmed my palm with a tender kiss. I stared at her a long time, and I knew then that I had, over the years, grown close to her in a way that disturbed me. I had always thought of her and Fred as my sister and brother; but now, looking at her perhaps for the last time, I grew wary. I cleared my throat, and said, "I don't know if I want to go through with this. I feel ill-at-ease. I have refrained from interviewing any of my close friends. The things I want to know are too emotional, too personal, too intimate, too highly charged."

"I know, Fred told me how exciting it was," she said, touching my hand.

"I want the truth, your truth. And if there's anyone

157

who'll tell me the truth I believe it's you. Fred sure did."
I smiled.

"Well, I haven't become chicken. I'm all for it. Anyway, I'll be on a boat in a few hours." She laughed as if she were putting something over on somebody. "So you'd better begin."

Again I cleared my throat, looked through my notes, and read off a question. *Have you ever, in any way at all, felt sexually aroused or sexually proud as a black woman because Fred is a white man—I mean, because his skin is white? Does that excite you, is it persistent in your relationship? Would you talk about it, one way or the other?*

Jesus. I guess so. Secretly, I mean. Like when he's naked I like to watch him when he's not looking. In my mind I think of him as white, or when we make love. . . . I try to vision his body without his color, but that never works. You just can't think of a man without him having some kind of characteristics, physical, I mean—a man is fat or tall or regal or brown or black. . . . Fred's white and that's the way I see him. He does the same thing too. I know he does, he's told me many times that he likes my color, my blackness . . . it excites him. . . . I play with him sometimes; I prance around in the nude pretending I'm not aware that he's watching. It makes you feel good because somebody loves you because you're black; most people don't, you know. In public? . . . Well, I feel proud . . . I mean, after all, I'm not ashamed because Fred's white. What? I don't know . . . I mean, well I've never really thought about it; but now that you've mentioned it, I believe I do, or I have, a tendency, that is, to feel a little better or superior—no, no, not superior, but just a little better than other Negro women. I feel they envy me, and I like it. . . . Damn, I never really analyzed that before.

Would you say, or can you say, because Fred is a white man that was the main reason you married him, or the main reason you fell in love with him? Would you say that, or have you ever felt that way?

I'll answer that by saying that if Fred messed up tomorrow —and I found out, of course—I'd leave him. I don't love him because he is white. I love him and married him because he's got good qualities (good for me, you know, good according to my standards), and those qualities have nothing to do with his whiteness. Yet, he is white, and as I said, I find myself appreciating myself because a white man married me, fell in love with me . . . I suppose. I'm no nut: I don't want a man just because of his color alone, black or white. Nobody can force me to do it. As you know, Fred and I met in college, we started going together. I didn't like him at first, I think I must have been prejudiced. No, I was afraid of what people would say. . . . Fred did all the pursuing. I didn't run after him. He wooed me and proposed to me like any man is supposed to do. He loves me, I know, because I'm a Negro. But he loves me because of other things too. I feel the same way.

When you and Fred were courting and even after you got married, how did your friends treat you, did you notice any change, did anybody say anything, good or bad? Would you talk about that?

Not from my friends, but people in general. . . . I had to get used to them staring at us and making funny cracks, and— What kind? . . . things like, Am I being satisfied? and other intimidating remarks. Mostly by Negro men. If I'm at a party or something, and they find out I'm Fred's wife, they might whisper a remark in my ear. They're jealous. But I know how to handle them, and Fred too is not anybody's punk. Negro women tend to identify with me, some of them—a lot look mean at me. White women and white men try not to show any signs at all, but I can tell. . . . The men, some of them, when they see me with Fred, try to play up to me; the women don't like it, they get jealous and real silent. They give me tight, polite smiles, except the ones who don't have anything against mixed marriages. Oh, yes—my roommate, my best friend, didn't like me going with Fred. She'd do little things to prevent me from seeing him or to make me late for a date. She changed, but we still were friends. Some Negro women play up to me like something crazy. They ask me about sex with Fred. I never answer their questions, unless they're my closest friends—but, I've learned not to do that lately, because I had to almost curse several of them out when I found out that they wanted to make Fred—and just because I had him. My parents?—they love him, my mother especially. But Father, he pretends—he really can't seem to get it through his head that I'm grown and married. He's never really accepted Fred. He was against the marriage. And at the reception he wouldn't speak to Fred until I made him. And he's been trying to persuade me not to follow Fred to Europe. But he goes along anyway. . . .

You spoke about how you "visioned" Fred, naked, white, and so forth. And you said that he has told you he likes your blackness. Well—can you answer this? Has either of you ever said anything racial while you're making love? Does it excite or does it take away? You don't have to reply unless you want to.

May I have a drink?

Thanks. I've been thinking. And I don't know what to say, I mean how to say it. I think I know what you're driving at. Let's see . . . well, hell, all right. Yes. Wait, don't get me wrong. It's racial but not racist. At first I was scared to get angry. I might call him a white bastard or something. Funny thing, so was he. We were tense at first. Then one day we were arguing about something, I don't know what now, just a fight between husband and wife, and he called me a black bitch! Well, that did it. We called each other names for an hour. It was just what we needed. We had been trying to ignore each other's color—pretending that we had no color. After that, we realized something—that the greatest gift we had was our colors. No, no, wait, let me go on. I want to explain, at least, the way I feel. Fred's whiteness is just one more of his physical characteristics. I don't see why, just because of this messed-up society, I have to ignore those characteristics. Sure, I cry out to him, "Love me, white baby," just as I might cry out to you, "Love me, brown baby." And it would mean nothing more or less than that, that is, if I loved you and were moved to say that. People are drawn to each other because of all kinds of things; one of them is the physical characteristics. . . . Fred might call me his black stallion. He's not racist, he doesn't have an ounce of racism in him. I love him because he's a man. What's a man?—a bastard, a prick, a dog, so on. All right, a *white* dog or a *white* angel . . . a *black* nigger or a *black* nymph —a person can tell when something is spoken out of the excitement of love over against the excitement of hatred. I think that funny guy Dick Gregory has shown us all a great deal of joy and pleasure in making fun out of what most people are so tense and tight-mouthed about—all this race business. Your book is on race and sex. So I'm telling you, *yes, we get excited and might say anything.* So what!—we're lovers.

Do you consider yourself normal, or healthy? Have you or Fred ever had psychiatric care?

Normal? If you mean, am I like the "average Joe Blow" in the streets—the answer is, no. The average American is stupid; he's got a television mentality. He's backward; especially when it comes to race—or sex and race. I didn't marry Fred because I'm abnormal. I've never been to a psychiatrist and neither has he. I've been intimate with Negro men and other white men—I love Fred because he inspired it in me more than any other man I've known. And we're no beatniks. But you know all of this. . . .

I want it from your mouth. Tell me—this friend of yours, the roommate who opposed your relationship with Fred, did you ever notice any sort of homosexual or lesbian tendencies in her with reference to you?

How did you know?

And your father . . .

What about him?

Well, are you his baby? I mean, why—honestly—why do you suppose he has such a block against accepting Fred as his son-in-law?

I don't know. He never seemed to be prejudiced at all. But, you know, when it hits you right in your own backyard, I guess one's true feelings come out then.

Do you know any other—couples—Negro women and white men, married or just going together? Would you say they were typical of you and Fred?

Typical? Yes and no. They are all kinds. Some of them are pretty messed-up—you know, with race and all. That's all they talk about, sex; it's pretty indecent. There's one girl who hates Negroes so much until I wonder how she can stand herself. She is always talking about how better white men are than Negro men are . . . and she's always trying to get me to agree. I don't bother with her much. Then too, she cheats on the guy. And she embarrasses him in public. She's paranoid.

162

She thinks Negroes hate her because she's living with a white man . . . she's always provoking scenes. You know who I'm talking about, don't you. . . .

If something should happen, theoretically, such that you and Fred should break up, would you consider another white man?

Yes. Wait. I mean, I'm not stuck on white men. I meant, if I fall in love with a white man and he wants to marry me, I'll do it the same as I'd do it with a Negro or anybody else. And I know why you asked that. And the *real* answer to the *real* question is, yes, I can love a black man as soon as I can love a white one—it depends on what the Negro or the white man has to offer. Whooo!—it's getting late.

We took a taxi to the pier. "One more question, please. There's something I would like you to comment on," I said, and I avoided her eyes. "You said that you have been intimate with both Negro and white men. Tell me—is there any truth in the notion that blacks are larger or bigger than whites?"

Her laughter filled the taxi. The driver looked back. When she settled down, she said, "What's a big penis? How do you *measure* a big one? How many inches? What is the circumference?" She was laughing again. "Maybe I've had bad luck with Negroes. There's all sizes and colors. Fred's all right with me. He's pretty big, whatever *big* means. He thinks he could compete with anybody. And you know what?—so do I."

The huge vessel made a long noise like a mammoth foghorn. She kissed me quickly, and moved through the departure gate.

. . . .

163

There is no consistent background or personality configuration by which we can isolate black women who marry or who become intimate with white men. Some of them are from well-bred northern backgrounds; some are from the South, poor and uneducated; some are rather dark and "unattractive"; others are light and sophisticated or dark and sophisticated. They run from such assorted personality types, backgrounds, and occupations as Lorraine Hansberry (playwright), Charlayne Hunter (first black coed, University of Georgia), Eartha Kitt (entertainer and actress), right on down to common laborers, domestics, mere housewives, and schoolteachers such as Hilda and others like or unlike her. A few are products of mixed marriages themselves. The only thing common to them all before they become intimate with white men is that they move in circles where they might, accidentally or deliberately, be approached by a white man.

For instance, one informant, who was not married to but who had a child by a white man, grew up in a section of the Bronx where few black people lived. She was surrounded by whites, mostly Jews. Consequently, she dated white boys, and when she became pregnant, the boy's parents prevented him from marrying her. This informant seemed to think that in the North, as in the South, black women are often the victims of sexual exploitation by white men—white men who will have sex with black women but who will not marry them. This informant was bitter and disillusioned. She stated that she would never become intimate with a white man again. She had this to say regarding the exploitation of black women in the North by white men:

It is hard as hell to force a white man to marry you, no matter what part of the country you are in. In the North, white men take advantage of spade women just as much as they do in the South . . . I know. I've worked in the garment district of New York. The bosses and the foremen and the men in general blackmail Negro and Puerto Rican women into sex with them before they will give jobs or raise salaries or other little handouts. And what can the women do—they have to work, they need money, they want attention and favors. . . .

In the North, certain bars and coffeehouses (especially in Greenwich Village), liberal organizations such as CORE, NAACP, the schools and universities, mixed social and political functions, or any integrated situation, provide opportunities for a black woman to be approached by a white man.

Although few, if any, African-American women will admit it, in those who are suffering from grave feelings of racial inferiority, the desire to escape from a despised self is part of the reason why they become intimate with white men. I have found, time after time, that black women who secretly hate their race are apt to end up in the arms of a white lover. There is also the wish to have light-skinned children, or to actually have a white baby. Although the white boy refused to marry her, the informant I mentioned above went ahead, against the advice of parents and friends, and gave birth to the child, because, in her words, she "wanted to show the world and the father the kind of bastard the white man is. I also wanted that child because someday the world will have to reckon with him as a human being and as a product of a mixed corelationship."

The black woman in the North perceives the white man in largely the same terms as she does in the South. He is a prestige figure. To capture him is to enhance the sexual ego of the black woman. In many instances, it represents "getting back" at white women and rising above other black females. The white man, according to white standards, is handsomer than most blacks. He has a better job, he moves in more refined circles, and, as almost every black woman will admit, he is less demanding and less prone to violence than the black man. "White men don't complain about cleaning the house, cooking on time, or about any other things that our men do," stated one black woman who was very hostile towards black men. "My first old man was black," she went on, "and all we did was fuss and fight. From sunup to sundown, it was a nigger this and a nigger that. We got divorced, and I married my present husband. He treats me so different, so kind and understanding. Anything I say goes. He worships the ground I walk on. . . ."

Repeatedly I have witnessed black women virtually dominating their white husbands. There may be fights, but the usual winner is the woman. She capitalizes on her Negroness and on her sex image by wielding a sort of Amazon mastery over the white male. In all but a few black woman-white man relationships, it is the man who must do the adjusting—and what he must adjust to is nothing less than what is referred to as the Negro's "mode of existence," or the Negro's conceptualization of life in the United States. I have observed this in many ways and upon innumerable occasions in the relationship between Hilda and Fred.

Like many white women who become intimate with black men, many black women are latent or unconscious homosexuals—the white man's color and unfamiliarity tend to heighten or excite their sense of themselves as females. Such women simply cannot get along with black men. In many instances, since he is considered kind, gentle, and compliant, the white man may psychosexually represent a pseudo-female for an otherwise homosexual, or lesbian-inclined, black woman. Again, like many white women, a black woman may turn to the white man merely because she cannot do any better. The males of her own race may consider her too "black and ugly" for their attention; while a liberal white man who is free of the influence of the white standards of beauty, or a white man who is simply pornographically excited by Negro women, will pursue her and even marry her.

The intense strain of forever having to justify and defend (to whites and blacks alike) one's intimacy with a white man has driven some black women to chronic paranoia. In addition to being under the constant scrutiny of others, the black woman, no matter how "liberated" she may be, is a victim of the ideology of sex-and-race in America, and is therefore under the perpetual scrutiny of her own conscience as well. Day by day she must not only encounter the stares and intimidating innuendoes of other people, she must also grapple with her own inner guilt—she must justify her interracial relationship to herself! The fact that she *loves* her spouse is not enough. On the contrary, it is this fact that often intensifies the guilt—for everybody knows that a black woman is not supposed to fall in love with a white man! Consequently, the particular woman grows nervous and defensive whenever she and her white man are in public or are around other people—whites as well as blacks. She is always on guard for the slightest off-key remark. The stress of living in a state of constant anxiety creates in the social personality of a few black women a passion for punishing themselves—they suspect everybody, especially white women and black men, of hating them for marrying a white man. Out of their desire to defend themselves, out of inner guilt, these women overreact to almost everyone and everything. Acting out of fantasy, they provoke a situation in reality where they and their white men usually end up embarrassed, not to mention the embarrassment experienced by those upon whom these women have projected their anxiety.

On the other hand, anxiety does not emanate out of nothing; paranoia is not a product of thin air. There are people in the world who will hate, degrade, intimidate, and accuse of a moral crime anyone who becomes involved in a personal relationship that crosses the color line. The disturbing thing is to analyze the motives and the sexual fiber of those who do the accusing, hating, and intimidating, or of those who endeavor to prevent black women from marrying or courting a white man, and vice versa. The reader will recall Hilda's roommate, who tried in various ways to frustrate Hilda's relationship with Fred. She showed lesbian tendencies towards Hilda. Hilda further stated that her roommate showed signs of jealousy, envy, and finally hatred for Fred, who was not only a man but a *white* man. Fred's being white made it impossible for Hilda's roommate to identify with Fred in his relationship with Hilda. During the course of my investigation and research, several cases of this sort came to my attention. I suspect that in many more cases than I encountered, homosexual envy constitutes the main motive for a woman's best friend opposing that woman's relationship with a man of the opposite race.

Like the white man who cannot bear the thought of his daughter marrying a black man, there is the black father who cannot accept the thought of his daughter marrying a Caucasian male. In both cases—black fathers and brothers and white fathers and brothers—the opposition springs from a deep sister- or daughter-incest urge. We, in America, want our sisters and daughters to marry some man with whom we feel we can sexually identify in the act of coitus with our sisters and daughters. I believe, for instance, that Hilda suspected something of this nature when I inquired about her father's inability to accept Fred as his son-in-law, and that it cut her too deeply. Therefore, she turned my question off with a short, snappy reply which sounded like a rationalization.

The majority of whites think of black women as predominantly "sluts." Lurking behind this label is the obvious sexual connotation: white men and women and blacks, too, prepare to make indecent overtures and insinuations instantly when they see a black woman with a white man. Barbara McNair, because of her role as successor to Diahann Carroll in the musical play *No Strings*, where she portrayed a black girl in Paris having an affair with a white man, received numerous letters questioning and impugning her virtue as a woman. Most of these letters were from sexually jealous white women.[14] But they might also have come from blacks. When Charlayne Hunter married her husband, storms of "protest" letters poured in, a great many from blacks who thought that Miss Hunter had "sold out to the white man" or that she had "let the race down." And no doubt, many black men and women are burning with the question, if they have not already asked it, of whether Miss Hunter is "being satisfied"!

It is no surprise—and yet it is—that no black woman who marries or who "goes with" a white man thinks of herself as a "slut," or thinks she is mentally deformed or that she has "let the race down." Yet there is evidence that such questions eat at her conscience incessantly.

Out of the dark annals of man's inhumanity to woman, the epic of the black woman's ordeal in America is yet to be written. Finally, after nearly four centuries of oppression, having been raped, murdered, lynched, spit upon, pushed through back doors, denied human respect, thought of and treated as sluts and mammies and Negresses, fit only to breed and suckle babies, to wash and cook and scrub and sweat, after having been sexually depersonalized and taken bodily for the having, the black women of the modern era are just beginning to be recognized as human beings, as sexual creatures clothed in their own personal skins, as American citizens with public rights and duties, private longings and desires, like any other citizen of this republic. But the change is just beginning, and the beginning is fraught with hazards.

[14] *Look*, December 17, 1962.

More and more African-American women are being accepted into the mainstream of American society. In politics, in business, in the professions, in the field of labor, in government services, in entertainment, black women are making inroads. In fact, with the seemingly unmitigated attack on this society by contemporary blacks to let them in, the black woman, in many instances, is being accepted more readily than the black male. Specifically, in the area of fair employment, black women can obtain relatively decent jobs when, frequently, black men are turned away. Not yet so much in the South, but in the most liberal parts of the North, such as Washington, D.C., New York, and even Chicago, this is so. The black woman, then, is becoming economically self-sufficient. And this means, among other things, she is getting in a position where *she*, rather than the man, can do the *choosing* when it comes to what kind of man she is going to take for a husband or a lover.

Of course, it is no mystery why white society is now tending to accept the black woman more readily than the black male. First of all, the black woman, like the white woman, does not represent to the white world as much of an aggressor against the present power structure as does the black man. Then too, if, as a consequence of integration, the black woman should marry a rich white man's son (or any white man), the power still remains in the hands of the white man. Not so, if black males start marrying the bosses' daughters.

There is always the possibility of the white man wooing or perhaps overcoming his long-repressed desire for black females, especially if they are there alongside him in an office, a plant, or what have you. Indeed, the black

171

woman, like any other woman, is not going to let a "good opportunity" go to waste for long. And precisely because the black woman has been the low female on the Western World's esthetic beauty chart for so long, the love and admiration of a white man might be more appealing, fulfilling, and inspiring to her ego needs as a female than many of us can imagine. Because of this, more and more black men are beginning to vent hostility not upon the white man, but upon the black woman, especially those who are successful and who might show some interest in the white male.

When it comes to women, the black male, like the white male, is a product and a victim of male supremacy, and he becomes disgruntled and difficult to get along with if "his women" are in a position where they no longer have to honor his claim to superiority. In addition to the general crisis occurring in contemporary race relations, a more specific crisis is ensuing in the relations between black men and black women—and, I suspect, it will become more intense as time goes on unless black women (I say women because, in this regard, I doubt the capacity of the men) initiate measures to resolve it.

SIX

The Sociology of Sex and Racism in America

Implications for the Future

It is important to point out that this book is *not* called *Sex and Race in America*. It is called *Sex and Racism in America*. There is a world of difference between "race" and "racism."

"Race" is a *biological* term. It is a scientific *construct* whereby men may be classified into more or less exclusive groups on the basis of similarities and dissimilarities of physical characteristics. Races, according to one scholar, constitute the "existence of groups presenting certain similarities in somatic (biological or physical) characteristics which set them off from any other group and whose characteristics are transmitted and perpetu-

173

ated according to the laws of biological inheritance (or through the genes)."[1]

The characteristics whereby men are classified into races are physical, and *only* physical, and such physical traits are biologically inherited, that is, passed on from generation to generation by way of the genes. The most reliable physical characteristics employed by scientists in classifying men into races are: color of eyes; color, texture, and quantity of hair (including body hair); cranial formation; nasal index; body stance; facial structure; and pigmentation. On the bases of these characteristics, scientists have classified all of mankind into three broad categories. They are: 1) Mongoloid, 2) Negroid, 3) Caucasoid. There may be subclassifications, depending upon whether or not one includes variations of physical characteristics within each of the three broad racial groups; but such "splitting of hairs" has little or no scientific meaning. In fact, practically all modern scientists have virtually abandoned the business of classifying mankind into races, for they have come to the conclusion that there is but one race—and it is, as Ruth Benedict has so aptly put it, the human race.

Nobody can be classified into a race on the basis of such things as behavior patterns, personality type, mannerisms, intelligence, style of living, and so on; for, although these things may be passed on from generation to generation, they are passed on through the *learning* process, and *not* by way of birth. One does not biologically inherit good manners or a particular way of walking. For instance, if a child makes gestures while talking

[1] Juan Comas, "Racial Myths," *The Race Question in Modern Science* (UNESCO [Paris: M. Blondin, 1956]), p. 18.

that are similar to his father's gestures, the child did not come by this through inheritance. He learned such behavior from being around his father. He consciously or unconsciously *imitated* his father until his father's behavior traits became a part of the child's behavior. Nobody inherits a personality; *all behavior is learned.* Any baby anywhere can learn one language as readily as he can another, provided he is taught that language or, better yet, if he is in an environment where the language is spoken.

What about blood? Two things: 1) physical traits are not transmitted from one person to another through the blood; 2) behavior is not inherited through the blood. There is no known scientific way (or any other way) to distinguish the blood of one race from another, for the simple reason that there are no properties in the blood that are racial. Genes and chromosomes are the only proven factors that structure physical characteristics, and they are not to be found anywhere in the blood. "If there is inheritance by blood how are we to explain why children of the same parents differ in character when the *same* blood runs in their veins."[2]

And what about the "pure" race? If ever there were a pure race, it existed so long ago in history, even prehistory, that it matters naught that it ever existed. Juan Comas, an authority on race, states that there is no "pure" race; never has been . . . [3] Of "mongrelization," Ashley-Montagu, a scholar on the subject, writes:

[2] Ibid., p. 22.
[3] Ibid., p. 18.

In all the regions in which an advanced culture is found there has been conquest of one people or peoples by others. The claim that cross-breeds are degenerate is refuted by the actual fact that the whole population of the world is hybrid and becoming increasingly so.[4]

Again, Comas is pertinent:

The mixing of races has been going on since the very beginning of human life on earth.[5]

He further states that, as far as we know, there is no proof that crossbreeding produces degeneracy in the descendants of mixed parents.

In fact, history testifies to the contrary—that ". . . the conditions which allow of any group playing an important role in civilization are promoted by crossing with other races."[6]

Blacks are reputed to have larger penises than whites, and to be generally more virile than whites. These are said to be "racial traits," proving that they are more savage than and inferior to whites. But, as the psychologist Gordon Allport has suggested, it is not the actual size of the black's genitals that whites think they are describing; it is the *psychological* size. I further suggest that the "big penis" stereotype has something to do with the color of the black man's genitals—they, of course, are black. But suppose it were true or half-true that they are larger. Whites, I believe categorically, have longer and more hair on their heads and bodies than blacks, and it is more "animal-like" than that of blacks. Is this a sign

[4] M. F. Ashley-Montagu, *The Myth of Blood* (1943), p. 24.

[5] Comas, op. cit., p. 18.

[6] Ashley-Montagu, op. cit., p. 26.

of the white man's inherent "savagery," his evolutionary kinship to the anthropoid ape?

The painstaking investigations of the social psychologist Otto Klineberg, have led him to make the following statement: "There is no known physical characteristic that automatically translates itself into psychological or behavioral differences such as intelligence, pride, thrift, morality, and so on. There are no known characteristics that automatically produce inferior or superior status." If so, why has status got to be legislated, enforced by law as well as by public and private violence? If the African-American's reputed inferiority is so "natural," Americans would not have to worry about keeping him in "his place"; he would remain on the bottom rung of society out of his "natural" depravity.[7]

Everybody on this planet starts out at birth predominantly in the same significant fashion—*naked*. What happens to a person from then on is to a great extent a function of the forces operating in the society in which he must struggle to achieve manhood. The forces that, from birth to the grave, cripple, deform, deprave, neuroticize, and maim the African-American are *not* inherent in the identifiable features of the African-American's biological inheritance—his race. What makes race a problem in the United States is, rather, what we *make* out of the African-American's features, the way we *behave* toward anyone exemplifying "Negro" physical characteristics, and the way we *force* the African-American to behave toward himself and toward whites. It is our political, economic, and social (sexual) *ideology* to-

[7] Otto Klineberg, "Race and Psychology," *The Race Question in Modern Science* (UNESCO [Paris: M. Blondin, 1956]), pp. 55–57.

177

ward anyone having Negroid physical characteristics that *makes* race a problem in the United States. It is not race that makes a white man tremble on seeing a black man with a white woman; it is *racism*.

Racism is a man-made, man-enforced phenomenon. Nobody, not even the Southerner, is *born* a racist. Racism may be defined as *all of the learned behavior and learned emotions on the part of a group of people towards another group whose physical characteristics are dissimilar to the former group; behavior and emotions that compel one group to conceive of and to treat the other on the basis of its physical characteristics alone, as if it did not belong to the human race.* People learn to discriminate, learn to segregate, learn to believe that whites are better than blacks, learn to think and fear that black men want to rape white women, learn to think of and to treat black females as though they were animals. When people live in a society where such things are formally and informally taught and learned, and are practiced, it is inescapable that the ideology of racism does become a functional institution, organically interwoven with every other ideology and institution of that society. Thus, racism in America is as much a part of the "American way of life" as Protestantism or Big Business. I am referring to our social structure; our economic and political system; and the way power, jobs, and life opportunities are distributed in America on the basis of physical characteristics. When racism disappears, the nature of the American politico-economic system—the way power and jobs and the chances for the good life are distributed—will have changed.

What I am driving at is this: the racism of sex in

America and its effect upon the sexual behavior and attitudes between, as well as within, the races is not only "in the mind" of the people, but stems from and is maintained by an economic-political-social system that has made it and still makes it *profitable* for the majority of white Americans.

Throughout this book I have analyzed and discussed the personality of whites and the personality of the blacks, with a specific focus on sex. Personality does not float in thin air, and it does not emanate out of a vacuum. Personality is a product and a reflection of society, and it is in the social structure that one must look for the ultimate cause and the ultimate solution. *The racism of sex in the United States is but another aspect of the unequal political and economic relations that exist between the races in the American democracy.*

In the South the caste system (segregation, discrimination, interracial-marriage prohibitions, etc.) serves to maintain and promote, among other things, the sexual exploitation of black women by white men. Because of the law against intermarriage, southern white men are at liberty to impregnate black women without the women having any legal recourse for the protection of their illicit offspring or themselves. White women who know (or suspect) that their husbands are having relations with black females are virtually helpless also. In the crossfire of this situation stands the black male—he can be lynched for merely looking at a white woman in some places in the South. He can also be falsely accused and jailed, if not lynched, if a white woman desires to have relations with him and he refuses to comply.

179

Over a half-century ago, George Cable, the southern liberal of his time wrote:

Nationalization without racial confusion is ours to profess and to procure. . . . We cannot hold American principles in perfect faith and not do it. . . . To make national unity without hybridity—the world has never seen it done as we have got to do it.[8]

At the time Cable wrote this, at least 50 percent of the black population in the South was "hybrid." Today, 80 percent or more of the African-Americans in America have "white blood" in their veins. It is no wonder that many foreigners view Americans as hypocrites. When it comes to hypocrisy, the South is far more advanced than any other part of the nation. But the South has never claimed to uphold the principles of democracy in regard to the Negro. Sexually, the southern white man has mixed (and is mixing) almost at will with black women. What he has proclaimed is that black men and white women shall not mix. By and large, this has been (and is) the white man's sexual proclamation for the entire nation.

With the coming of modern contraceptives, however, and with the changes taking place in our attitudes towards having children, one must be cautious about any statistics regarding interracial sex in America. One can say, from the evidence at hand, that, as the social, economic, and political barriers that have traditionally separated whites and blacks continue to disappear, both the concrete and the psychological barriers between their

[8] George W. Cable, *The Negro Question* (Garden City, New York: Doubleday Anchor Books, 1958), pp. 117–18.

social (sexual) activities will also diminish. This can be seen in the parts of the North where integration is becoming more and more of a fact. However, before intermarriage becomes generally acceptable (especially between black men and white women), I am afraid there will be a bloody war.

When we consider interracial sex within the context of the African-American's eventually becoming integrated into the American democracy, we cannot, as Cable did, deny the fact that mixed marriages will become more common. Everybody, except the Southerner, denies that "integration and equal rights" will lead to intermarriage. While the denial is understandable, I am afraid it functions mainly to counteract the dangerous effects that such an admission would have upon the civil rights movement. And while the denial no doubt reflects sincerity on the part of the African-American, it does not take cognizance of the fact that there will be no way (from within the race or from without) to prevent intermarriage when black people become totally and completely integrated.

At present, the inroads that blacks are making into American society are slowly but surely transforming the entire social structure of America as it is related to the concept of democracy. Every American is aware, or ought to be aware, of the political and economic changes that will be and are being wrought in our lives by the so-called "Negro revolution." I find it impossible to believe that this revolution will stop short of effecting changes in the mode of our social relations between black and white. People do not "integrate" in any area of activity

181

without, after a while, giving in to the human pressure to "find out" about each other, to talk to each other, to grow fond of each other, and eventually to *desire* each other. *Integration will not necessarily "lead to" intermarriage; but it will definitely make intermarriage more universally possible.* And this, in turn, will make democracy more universally applicable.

I am not implying that black men and women are possessed by "an ungovernable sexual craving for white flesh." If blacks have an urge to marry whites, it is as much a *social* urge as it is sexual—perhaps even more so. Oliver C. Cox, an African-American sociologist, has stated that when blacks want white people it is not for sexual reasons alone, but for their importance as vehicles in the African-American's struggle for economic and cultural position.[9]

"Assimilation" is the process of interpenetration and fusion of the habits, customs, traditions, and historical backgrounds of different ethnic groups in such a way that their major cultural distinctions become synthesized into one culture, and the groups become more or less one people mutually sharing the privileges and responsibilities of a common society. This process has been going on throughout the entire span of human history. Not once, to my knowledge, has it happened without intermarriage ultimately taking place. In fact, intermarriage is perhaps the crucial test in determining when a people have completely won their way into the mainstream of any given society.

Granted—assimilation may be undesirable for most

[9] Oliver C. Cox, *Caste, Class, and Race* (New York: Monthly Review Press, 1959), p. 386.

whites and for most blacks. But in a supposedly democratic society, I do not see how blacks (or whites) can ever realize their ambition of becoming free men and women if, on the basis of race, they are still restricted by law, custom, and tradition, in one of the most private areas of their lives—the right to marry whoever will marry them. I do not see how the society itself can really be free, or democratic.

Most of all, I do not see how men, women, and children can grow and live healthy, productive lives in a world where—even if all other forms of racism and Jim Crow have disappeared—the racism of sex still prevails to plague, to distort, and to deprave the human conscience of blacks and whites alike.

About the Author

Calvin C. Hernton has published eight books. He is a poet, novelist, essayist, and social scientist and has taught black and African literature and creative writing at Oberlin College for over fifteen years.